(9609)

A Bibliography of Swift Studies: 1945–1965

A Bibliography of

Swift
Studies 1945–1965

Compiled by

James J. Stathis

Vanderbilt University Press

Nashville, Tennessee   1967

Copyright © 1967 by
Vanderbilt University Press

Composed and printed by Heritage Printers, Inc.,
Charlotte, North Carolina

Bound by Nicholstone Book Bindery
Nashville, Tennessee

Library of Congress Catalogue Card Number 67–17563

Printed in the United States of America

For My Parents

Preface

DURING THE TWO decades that have elapsed since the publication of the valuable bibliography of critical studies by Louis A. Landa and James E. Tobin, scholarly interest in Jonathan Swift has continued to accelerate. The following pages indicate that the number of studies treating Swift between 1945 and 1965 is proportionate to the number of studies that were published over the half century covered by Landa and Tobin. But more important is the knowledge that this greater attention to matters Swiftian has been accompanied by distinctly different critical and biographical emphases, with the result that we now have a much better understanding of Swift and his writings.

Since these new emphases are charted by Milton Voigt in his excellent study of *Swift and the Twentieth Century* (1964), no attempt is made here to discuss Swift scholarship. Annotation has been kept to a minimum. Titles are arranged alphabetically under six major categories, two of which are subdivided for the reader's convenience. Classification, however convenient, creates certain problems. For instance, should Ricardo Quintana's *Swift: An Introduction* be classified under General Criticism or Biography? And what of items that discuss several works? To obviate as far as possible the difficulties that must occompany any arbitrary arrangement, a system of cross-reference *by item numbers* has been added. Frequently, these references direct the reader's attention to similar, supporting, or opposing views.

This bibliography is intended to be comprehensive within certain limits only. A considerable number of unpublished dissertations and selected book reviews have been included. On the other hand, trade editions of Swift's works, editions of separate or selected works prepared for classroom use, anthologies and histories of English literature, popular writings intended for the general reader, with few exceptions, have been excluded. For those users who wish to add titles that they feel should be included, several blank pages are provided after the Index.

Although in such a work as this perhaps neither total accuracy nor completeness is possible, I hope that this compilation is both accurate and full enough to be useful both to the accomplished scholar and to the beginning student of Swift.

I wish to thank the Vanderbilt University Research Council for granting me the time and the financial assistance necessary to pursue my study of Swift, from which this bibliography developed. Miss Anne Alexander, Mrs. Marion Deitchman, and Mr. Eugene H. Scheppe have been most generous with their time in assisting me with various aspects of the bibliography. For his encouragement and always sound advice, I am grateful to my friend and colleague, Professor John M. Aden. My debt to Professor Ricardo Quintana is a life-long one, but I wish to acknowledge part of it at this time.

James J. Stathis
Vanderbilt University

Abbreviations

AHR	*American Historical Review*
AN&Q	*American Notes and Queries*
AUMLA	*Journal of the Australasian Universities Language and Literature Association*
BA	*Books Abroad*
BJRL	*Bulletin of the John Rylands Library*
BuR	*Bucknell Review*
CE	*College English*
DA	*Dissertation Abstracts*
EA	*Études Anglaises*
ELH	*Journal of English Literary History*
ELN	*English Language Notes*
HLB	*Harvard Library Bulletin*
HLQ	*Huntington Library Quarterly*
HR	*Hudson Review*
JEGP	*Journal of English and Germanic Philology*
JHI	*Journal of the History of Ideas*
LQ&HR	*London Quarterly and Holborn Review*
MLN	*Modern Language Notes*
MLQ	*Modern Language Quarterly*
MLR	*Modern Language Review*
MP	*Modern Philology*
N&Q	*Notes and Queries*

PBSA	*Papers of the Bibliographical Society of America*
PMLA	*Publications of the Modern Language Association of America*
PQ	*Philological Quarterly*
QQ	*Queens Quarterly*
REL	*Review of English Literature*
RES	*Review of English Studies*
SAQ	*South Atlantic Quarterly*
SB	*Studies in Bibliography*
SP	*Studies in Philology*
SR	*Sewanee Review*
SRL	*Saturday Review of Literature*
TLS	London *Times Literary Supplement*
TSE	*Tulane Studies in English*
TSL	*Tennessee Studies in Literature*
TSLL	*Texas Studies in Language and Literature*
UTQ	*University of Toronto Quarterly*
WHR	*Western Humanities Review*
WMQ	*William and Mary Quarterly*
YR	*Yale Review*

Contents

A Bibliography of Swift Studies: 1945–1965

I

Bibliography, Canon, Editions

A. Bibliography and Canon

Cambridge Bibliography of English Literature. Ed. George   [1]
Watson. V, (Supplement). Cambridge, England, 1957.

Davies, Godfrey. "A New Edition of Swift's 'The Story of the   [2]
Injured Lady'," *HLQ*, VIII (1945), 388–392.
    The four-page preface appended in 1749 adds an episode
to the work. Davies believes the author of the preface to be
Charles Lucas, an Irish patriot who wished to inform George
II of certain Irish wrongs.

Davis, Herbert. "The Manuscript of Swift's Sermon 'On Broth-   [3]
erly Love'," in *Pope and His Contemporaries: Essays Presented to George Sherburn* (Edited by James L. Clifford and
Louis A. Landa). Oxford, 1949, pp. 147–158.
    Suggests that the autographed manuscript in Trinity Col-
lege, Dublin, provides conclusive evidence that Swift was
describing his own sermon practice in his advice concerning
the method of preparing a sermon.

———. "The Manuscripts of Swift's 'Directions to Servants',"   [4]
in *Studies in Art and Literature for Belle da Costa Greene*

(Edited by Dorothy Miner). Princeton, N.J., 1954, pp. 433–444.
Makes comparisons and discusses internal evidence.

Dearing, Vinton A. "Jonathan Swift or William Wagstaffe?"   [5]
HLB, VII (1953), 121–130.
Claims the *Miscellaneous Works of Dr. William Wagstaffe* (1726) for Wagstaffe.

Ehrenpreis, Irvin, and James L. Clifford. "Swiftiana in Rylands   [6]
English MS. 659 and Related Documents," *BJRL*, XXXVII (1955), 368–392.
Describes and reprints this collection of twenty-five items.
See Mayhew (23).

English Literature, 1660–1800: A Bibliography of Modern Stud-   [7]
ies (Edited by R. S. Crane, *et al.*). 4 vols. Princeton, N.J., 1950–1962.
For the years after 1962, see the annual July issue of *PQ*.

Ferguson, Oliver W. "Swift, Tisdall, and 'A Narrative'," *N&Q*,   [8]
CXCVIII (1953), 485–486.
Suggests that this anti-Presbyterian tract is by William Tisdall not Swift.

———. "The Authorship of 'Apollo's Edict'," *PMLA*, LXX   [9]
(1955), 433–440.
Claims the poem for Mrs. Mary Barber.

Friends of the Library of Trinity College, Dublin. *Catalogue*   [10]
of the Exhibition Held in the Library from October 19 to
November 23, 1945, to Commemorate the Bicentenary of the
Death of Jonathan Swift. Dublin, 1945.
See Hayward (13), Wiley (45), and Williams (48).

Fussell, Paul, Jr. "Speaker and Style in *A Letter of Advice to a* [11] *Young Poet* (1721), and the Problem of Attribution," *RES*, X (1959), 63–67.

"When we focus on questions of speaker and style, we perceive in *A Letter of Advice* ... the work of a consummately skilled dramatic parodist, a dramatic parodist so like Swift in every respect and every technical habit that it is incredible that Swift was not the author of the piece." See Davis (199).

Griffith, R. H. "Swift's 'Contests,' 1701: Two Editions," *N&Q*, [12] CXCII (1947), 114–117.

Considers printing practices. See Teerink (37).

[Hayward, John] *A Catalogue of Printed Books and Manu-* [13] *scripts, by Jonathan Swift, D.D., Exhibited in the Old Schools in the University of Cambridge. To Commemorate the 200th Anniversary of His Death, October 19, 1745.* Cambridge, England, 1945.

Reviewed by A. N. Wiley, *PQ*, XXV (1946), 167–169. See (10), Wiley (45), and Williams (48).

Horne, Colin J. "An Epitaph Attributed to Swift," *N&Q*, [14] CXCIX, N.S. I (1954), 525–527.

Transcribes the epitaph to Sir George Beaumont, (c. 1663–1737); it was attributed to Swift by John Nichols in his *History and Antiquities of the County of Leicester* (1798).

Jarrell, Mackie L. "A New Swift Attribution: The Preface to [15] Sheridan's Sermon on St. Cecilia's Day," *PMLA*, LXXVIII (1963), 511–515.

Argues from internal evidence that this short letter to Sheridan, signed "A. D.," may have been written by Swift.

Johnson, Maurice. "A Love Song. In the Modern Taste," *John-* [16] *sonian News Letter*, X (1950), No. 1, 4–5.

Suggests that Pope not Swift is the author.

Landa, Louis A., and J. E. Tobin. *Jonathan Swift: A List of* [17]
Critical Studies Published from 1895 to 1945, to Which Is
Added "Remarks on Some Swift Manuscripts in the United
States" by Herbert Davis. New York, 1945.
    Reviews: *TLS*, April 6, 1946, p. 163; E. K. Gibson, *MLQ*,
VII (1946), 507; D. F. Bond, *MLN*, LXII (1947), 210–212;
A. W. Secord, *JEGP*, XLVI (1947), 222.

Leslie, Shane. "The Swift Manuscripts in the Morgan Library," [18]
in *Studies in Art and Literature for Belle da Costa Greene*
(Edited by Dorothy Miner). Princeton, N.J., 1954, pp. 445–
448.
    Finds the letters and poems in the Morgan Library to be
"brilliantly genuine."

Longe, Arthur. *The Old Night-Watchman, the Ghost of Spix-* [19]
worth Hall. Ipswich, England, 1950.
    Contains verses ascribed to Swift. See *TLS*, October 20,
1950, p. 667.

McCue, Daniel L., Jr. "A Newly Discovered Broadsheet of [20]
Swift's *Last Speech and Dying Words of Ebenezer Elliston*,"
HLB, XIII (1959), 362–368.
    A 1722 text and the only known separate edition.

Main, C. F. "Defoe, Swift, and Captain Tom," *HLB*, XI (1957), [21]
71–79.
    Argues for Defoe's authorship of the Captain Tom pam-
phlets, 1710–1711.

Mayhew, George P. "Swift's Anglo-Latin Games and a Frag- [22]
ment of *Polite Conversation* in Manuscript," *HLQ*, XVII
(1954), 133–159.
    Discusses the precision with which Swift caught and fixed

the banalities of his society's polite conversation. See Mayhew (23) and (29).

———. "Swift's Games with Language in Rylands English MS. [23] 659," *BJRL*, XXXVI (1954), 413–448. See Ehrenpreis and Clifford (6), Mayhew (22).

———. "Two Burlesque Invitations by Swift," *N&Q*, CXCIX, [24] N.S. I (1954), 55–57.
To John Rochfort.

———. "Swift's Manuscript Version of 'On His Own Deafness'," [25] *HLQ*, XVIII (1954), 85–87.
Indicates many differences from the printed text.

———. "A Draft of Ten Lines from Swift's Poem to John Gay," [26] *BJRL*, XXXVII (1954), 257–262.
The draft is printed.

———. "A Missing Leaf from Swift's 'Holyhead Journal'," [27] *BJRL*, XLI (1959), 388–413.
Analyzes Egerton MS. No. 201 in Swift's hand and claims that it was part of a journal Swift kept in 1727.

———. " 'Rage or Raillery': Swift's *Epistle to a Lady* and *On* [28] *Poetry: A Rhapsody*," *HLQ*, XXIII (1960), 159–180.
Discovers previously unnoticed versions in a volume of Faulkner's edition of Swift's *Works* (1735) at the Huntington Library.

———. "Two Entries of 1702–3 for Swift's *Polite Conversation*, [29] 1738," *N&Q*, CCVI, N.S. VIII (1961), 49–50.
Uses two entries in Forster No. 505; Swift began collecting material for that work in Ireland in 1702 or 1703. See Mayhew (22).

Powell, William S. "A Swift Broadside from the Opposition,"   [30]
Virginia Magazine of History and Biography, LXVII (1959),
164–169.
Claims the verses titled "The Loyal Address of the Clergy
of Virginia" (1702) for Swift.

Scouten, Arthur H. "Materials for the Study of Swift at the   [31]
University of Pennsylvania," *Library Chronicle of the Uni-
versity of Pennsylvania*, XXIII (1957), 47–52.
The Teerink collection.

——. "The Earliest London Printings of 'Verses on the Death   [32]
of Doctor Swift'," *SB*, XV (1962), 243–247.
Refutes Teerink (38); see also Teerink (39), Johnson
(361), Slepian (383), Waingrow (386).

Sherburn, George. "The 'Copies of Verses' about Gulliver,"   [33]
TSLL, III (1961), 3–7.
Written not by Pope but by the Scriblerians together.

Stephens, John C., Jr. " '7 Penny Papers of My Own'," *N&Q*,   [34]
CXCVII (1952), 139–140.
Claims that the *Letter of Thanks* is not one.

Teerink, Herman. "Swift's 'Cadenus and Vanessa'," *HLB*, II   [35]
(1948), 254–257.
See Teerink (36).

——. "Swift's 'Cadenus and Vanessa' Again," *HLB*, III (1949),   [36]
435–436.
See Teerink (35).

——. "Swift's *Discourse . . . Contests and Dissensions in Athens*   [37]
and Rome, 1701," *Library*, 5th series, IV (1949), 201–205.
Presents evidence that "there are indeed only two issues

or editions (and no more) to be distinguished as x and w." Other variant copies are "simply cross-combinations of x and w." See Griffith (12).

――. "Swift's 'Verses on the Death of Doctor Swift'," *SB*, IV   [38]
(1951), 183–188.
    See Scouten (32) for a different opinion; also Teerink (39), Johnson (361), Slepian (383), Waingrow (386).

――. " 'Verses on the Death of Doctor Swift' Again," *SB*, VII   [39]
(1954), 238–239.
    See Scouten (32), Teerink (38), Johnson (361), Slepian (383), Waingrow (386).

――. *A Bibliography of the Writings of Jonathan Swift.* Sec-   [40]
ond Edition, revised and corrected. (Edited by Arthur H. Scouten). Philadelphia, 1963.
    Reviews: G. P. Mayhew, *PQ*, XLIII (1964), 394–396; D. Foxon, *Book Collector*, XIII (1964), 379–380; D. P. French, *BA*, XXXVIII (1964), 317; R. C. Steensma, *CE*, XXV (1964), 477.

"The Virginia and Richard Ehrlich Collection," *Boston Public*   [41]
Library Quarterly, XII (1960), 103–109.
    Describes the Collection and mentions a note dated December 15, 1722, in which 'Jonath Swift Decan' notified his clergy of a chapter meeting at St. Patrick's.

"Thomas Tickell and *Thersites*," *Bodleian Library Record*, IV   [42]
(1953), 291.
    By Swift not Tickell.

Todd, William B. "Another Attribution to Swift," *PBSA*, XLV   [43]
(1951), 82–83.
    Argues that *On Taste. An Essay* (1732) was falsely attributed to Swift.

Webb, D. A. "Broadsides Relating to Swift," *Annual Bulletin,*   [44]
Friends of the Library of Trinity College, Dublin. Dublin,
1946, pp. 8–11.

Wiley, Autrey Nell. *Jonathan Swift, 1667–1745: An Exhibi-*   [45]
*tion of Printed Books at the University of Texas, October
19–December 31, 1945, Described by Autrey Nell Wiley.*
Austin, 1945.
  Reviews: J. Hayward, *MLR,* XLI (1946), 345; H. Williams,
RES, XXII (1946), 334; H. Teerink, *MLN,* LXII (1947),
429–430. See (10), Hayward (13), and Williams (48).

———. "Jonathan Swift: A Bicentennial Exhibition," *Library*   [46]
Chronicle of the University of Texas, II (1946), 17–20.

Williams, Sir Harold. "Deane Swift, Hawkesworth, and the   [47]
Journal to Stella," in *Essays on the Eighteenth Century Presented to David Nichol Smith* (Edited by J. R. Sutherland
and F. P. Wilson). Oxford, 1945, pp. 33–48.
  Attempts to establish the superiority of Deane Swift as
an editor in spite of the consensus that Hawkesworth is the
more reliable.

———. "Swift Exhibition at Cambridge," *TLS,* October 20,   [48]
1945, p. 504.
  See (10), Hayward (13), and Wiley (45).

Woolley, David. "The Canon of Swift," *Johnsonian News Let-*   [49]
ter, XX (1960), No. 2, 8.
  Claims for Swift the prose tract *A Modest Defense of a late
Poem, by an unknown Author, called the Lady's Dressing
Room. Written in the Year MDCCXXXII,* which appeared
in 1746 in volume 8 of Faulkner's edition. See Davis (353).

See (199), (204), (353), (354), (361), (380), (381), (409),
(521), (641), (650), (651).

B. Editions

The Correspondence of Jonathan Swift. Edited by Sir Harold   [50]
Williams. 5 vols. Oxford, 1963–1965.
   Reviews: D. P. French, *BA*, XXXVIII (1964), 436; R.
Paulson, *JEGP*, LXIII (1964), 792–795. See Donoghue (460)
and Hough (463).

An Enquiry into the Behavior of the Queen's Last Ministry.   [51]
Edited by Irvin Ehrenpreis. IUPHS, No. 36. Bloomington,
1956.
   Reviews: G. Davies, *PQ*, XXXVI (1957), 406–407; O. W.
Ferguson, *JEGP*, LVI (1957), 287–290; C. J. Horne, *MLR*,
LII (1957), 419; F. G. James, *AHR*, LXII (1957), 444; N. C.
Starr, *CE*, XIX (1957), 86; K. Williams, *RES*, IX (1958),
86–88.

Journal to Stella. Edited by Sir Harold Williams. 2 vols. Oxford,   [52]
1948.
   Reviews: *TLS*, January 31, 1948, p. 64; *QQ*, LV (1948),
226–227; H. Davis, *PQ*, XXVIII (1949), 405–407; E. Pons,
RES, XXV (1949), 364–367; G. Sherburn, *MLR*, XLIV
(1949), 113–114. See Pritchett (465) and Wilson (468).

The Poems of Jonathan Swift. Edited by Sir Harold Williams.   [53]
Second edition. 2 vols. Oxford, 1958.
   Reviews: I. Ehrenpreis, *MLR*, LIV (1959), 260–261; H.
Papajewski, *Anglia*, LXXIX (1962), 504–505.

The Collected Poems of Jonathan Swift. Edited with an Intro-   [54]
duction and Critical Comments by Joseph Horrell. 2 vols.
London, 1958.
   Reviews: *TLS*, May 30, 1958, pp. 302–303; M. Bewley,
Spectator, August 29, 1958, pp. 283–284; J. Raymond, *New
Statesman*, LV (1958), 735–736; M. Johnson, *PQ*, XXXVIII
(1959), 354; H. Buchan, *RES*, XII (1961), 88–89.

The Poems of Jonathan Swift. Edited with an Introduction by   [55]
Padraic Colum. New York, 1962.

Jonathan Swift: Polite Conversation. Edited with an Introduc-   [56]
tion, Notes, and Commentary by Eric Partridge. New York,
1963.
   Reviewed by J. Hollander, *New Statesman,* LXVI (1963),
110–111; R. I. McDavid, Jr., *PQ,* XLIII (1964), 393–394.

"Jonathan Swift's *Polite Conversation* with an Introduction   [57]
and Notes." Edited by Philip R. Micks. Unpublished dissertation, Columbia University, 1958.
   See *DA,* XX (1959), 1768–1769.

The Prose Writings of Jonathan Swift. Edited by Herbert   [58]
Davis. 14 vols. Oxford, 1939–1962. (Index in preparation).

I.   1696–1706. *A Tale of a Tub.* (1939).

II.   1706–1710. *Bickerstaff Papers and Pamphlets on the
     Church.* (1939).

III.   1710–1711. *The Examiner and Other Pieces.* (1940).

IV.   *A Proposal for Correcting the English Tongue, Polite
     Conversation, Etc.* (1957).
        Reviews: *TLS,* March 7, 1958, p. 129; M. Johnson,
     PQ, XXXVII (1958), 356–358.

V.   *Miscellaneous and Autobiographical Pieces.* (1962).
        Reviewed by G. Mayhew, *PQ,* XLII (1963), 379–
     381.

VI.   1711–1713. *Political Tracts.* (1951).
        Reviews: *TLS,* February 22, 1952, p. 144; I. Ehren-
     preis, *JEGP,* LI (1952), 599–601; R. Quintana, *PQ,*
     XXXI (1952), 306; H. Williams, *RES,* IV (1953), 185–
     186.

VII.   1713. *The History of the Last Four Years of the Queen.*
     (1951).
        Reviews: C. Tracy, *QQ,* LVIII (1951), 450–452;

I. Ehrenpreis, *PQ*, XXXI (1952), 303–305; I. Watt, *RES*, III (1952), 180–181.

VIII. 1713–1719. *Political Tracts.* (1953).
Reviews: G. Davies, *PQ*, XXXIII (1954), 303–304; H. Williams, *RES*, V (1954), 300–301.

IX. 1720–1723. *Irish Tracts and Sermons.* (1948).
Reviews: B. Dobrée, *Spectator*, July 16, 1948, p. 84; *TLS*, June 26, 1948, p. 361; J. C. Beckett, *Irish Historical Studies*, VI (1949), 228–229; A. Gewirth, *Ethics*, LIX (1949), 231; W. H. Irving, *SAQ*, XLVIII (1949), 622; H. Williams, *RES*, XXV (1949), 274–277.

X. 1724–1725. *The Drapier's Letters and Other Works.* (1941).

XI. 1726. *Gulliver's Travels.* (1941).

XII. 1728–1733. *Irish Tracts.* (1955).
Reviews: *TLS*, August 12, 1955, p. 458; O. W. Ferguson, *PQ*, XXXVI (1957), 408–410; C. J. Horne, *RES*, VIII (1957), 311–314.

XIII. 1733–1742. *Directions to Servants and Miscellaneous Pieces.* (1959).
Reviews: *TLS*, November 27, 1959, p. 695; D. P. French, *BA*, XXXV (1961), 392–393.

XIV. Index. In Preparation.

A Tale of a Tub, to which is Added, The Battle of the Books and the Mechanical Operation of the Spirit. Edited with an Introduction and Notes Historical and Explanatory by A. C. Guthkelch and D. Nichol Smith. Second Edition, Oxford, 1958.   [59]
Reviews: I. Ehrenpreis, *MLR*, LIV (1959), 89–90; *TLS*, March 7, 1959, p. 129.

See (477), (486).

II

Biography

"A Book from Swift's Library," *Bodleian Library Record*, III   [60]
(1951), 180–181.
  A copy of Virgil with Swift's own annotations. See Clarkson (73), Manly (116), and Williams (152).

Acworth, Bernard. *Swift.* London, 1947.   [61]
  Obviously intended for the general reader.

Babcock, R. W. "A Pilgrimage to Moor Park," *Dalhousie Review*, XXV (1945), 39–45.   [62]
  See (119).

Baker, Frank. "Jonathan Swift and the Wesleys," *LQ & HR*,   [63]
(October 1954), 290–300.
  Discusses what John Wesley and Swift had in common and family links between the two.

Barnds, William J. "Jonathan Swift, Preacher," *Anglican Theological Review*, XL (1958), 42–47.   [64]
  See Bennett (66), Gimblett (92), Landa (114), White (148), and Beckett (171).

Barrett, William. "Writers and Madness," *Partisan Review*, XIV   [65]
(January–February 1947), 5–22.

A highly imaginative psychoanalytic critique that sees
Swift well on the road to madness when he wrote *Gulliver.*
Among other things, "Swift wanted to be a horse, a beau-
tiful and gentle animal. . . ."

Bennett, Hiram R. "Jonathan Swift, Priest," *Anglican Theo-* [66]
logical Review, XXXIX (1957), 131–138.
   See Barnds (64), Gimblett (92), Landa (114), White (148),
and Beckett (171).

Bottome, Phyllis. "Is Neurosis a Handicap to Genius?" *Litera-* [67]
ture and Psychology, V (1955), 20–25.
   Contends that Swift's life and achievement support the
thesis "that neurosis must be the worst handicap genius has
ever had to face."

Brain, Sir Walter Russell. "The Illness of Dean Swift," *Irish* [68]
Journal of Medical Science, 6th series, (1952), 337–345.
   Finds it surprising that there has been so much discussion of
Swift's sanity "since he showed no symptoms suggesting
mental deterioration until he was over seventy years of age."
See Ehrenpreis (84), Wilson (156), (158), and (160).

Brookes, T. H. "Bi-centenary of Swift," *Contemporary Re-* [69]
view, CLXVIII (October 1945), 226–230.
   Aims "to glance at Swift as a man and as an ecclesiastic."

Brown, T. J. "English Literary Autographs: V. Jonathan [70]
Swift," *Book Collector*, II (1953), 100.
   Reproduces a sample.

Case, Arthur E. "Swift and Sir William Temple—a Conjecture," [71]
MLN, LX (1945), 259–265.
   Concerns Swift's own statements about the causes of his

deafness and giddiness and the date of his early visits to
Temple. See Ehrenpreis (78) and (86).

———. "Swift's Supposed Ingratitude Towards His Uncle God-   [72]
win: A Surmise," in *Pope and His Contemporaries: Essays
Presented to George Sherburn* (Edited by James L. Clifford
and Louis A. Landa). Oxford, 1949, pp. 129–134.
Discusses the question of Swift's dissatisfaction with the
education given him by his uncle Godwin.

Clarkson, Paul S. "Swift and Shakespeare," *N&Q*, CXCIII   [73]
(1948), 151.
Concerning Swift's library. See particularly Williams
(152); also (60), Manly (116).

Craig, Maurice James (Editor). *The Legacy of Swift: a Bi-*   [74]
centenary Record of St. Patrick's Hospital, Dublin. Dublin,
1948.
Includes a special exhibition catalogue.

Day, Robert A. "An Anonymous Attack on Swift," *N&Q*,   [75]
CC, N.S. II (1955), 530–532.
Presents the hypothesis that Mrs. Haywood prepared a col-
lection of high-flown letters dropping in allusions to the
Blounts and to Swift which were matters of common knowl-
edge.

Dennis, Nigel. *Jonathan Swift: A Short Character.* New York,   [76]
1964.
Reviews: P. Anderson, *Spectator*, November 19, 1965, p.
665; C. C. O'Brien, "The Dean's Identity," *New Statesman*,
LXX (1965), 1002; *TLS*, January 20, 1966, p. 44; W. K. Sey-
mour, *Contemporary Review*, July 1966, p. 52.

Drew, Elizabeth. *Literature of Gossip.* New York, 1964, pp.   [77]
43–66.

Ehrenpreis, Irvin. "Swift and Mr. John Temple," *MLN*, LXII   [78]
(1947), 145–154.
    See Case (71), Ehrenpreis (86).

———. "Swift's Father," *N&Q*, CXCII (1947), 496–498.   [79]
    See Ehrenpreis (86).

———. "Swift's Voyages," *MLN*, LXV (1950), 256–257.   [80]
    Swift made 16 voyages between England and Ireland be-
fore the end of 1704.

———. "Swift's April Fool for a Bibliophile," *Book Collector*, II   [81]
(1953), 205–208.
    A joke perpetrated by Swift on Sir Andrew Fountaine.

———. "Swift and Esther," *TLS*, January 8, 1954, p. 25.   [82]
    Concerns property transactions. See Jackson (102) and
O'Leary (131).

———. "The Pattern of Swift's Women," *PMLA*, LXX (1955),   [83]
706–716.
    Contends that Swift's attitude toward women has its origin
in his childhood—in the lonely life of a fatherless child. See
Hardy (99), Le Brocquy (115), Yost (162).

———. *The Personality of Jonathan Swift*. London and Cam-   [84]
bridge, Mass., 1958.
    Reviewed by H. Corke, *Encounter*, XI (October 1958),
84–87; *TLS*, August 15, 1958, p. 456; L. Landa, *PQ*, XXXVIII
(1959), 351–353; C. Ackerman, *CLA Journal*, III (1959), 126;
B. Fabian, *Archiv für das Studium der neuren Sprachen*,
CXCVI (1959), 206–207; C. J. Horne, *MLR*, LIV (1959),
595–596; G. Thomas, *English*, XII (1959), 144; H. Williams,
RES, XI (1960), 92–93. See Brain (68), Ehrenpreis (86),

Hardy (99), Le Brocquy (115), Wilson (158) and (160), Yost (162).

———. "Swift's Grandfather," *TLS*, June 12, 1959, p. 353.   [85]
   See Welply (147).

———. *Mr. Swift and His Contemporaries*. Volume One of   [86]
   Swift: The Man, His Works, and The Age. London and Cam-
   bridge, Mass., 1962.
   Reviewed by *TLS*, September 14, 1962, p. 690; O. W.
   Ferguson, *PQ*, XLII (1963), 375–377; J. C. Beckett, *Irish
   Historical Studies*, XIII (1963), 271–273; F. Brady, *YR*, LII
   1963), 267–270; G. Bullough, *English*, XIV (1963), 200–202;
   H. Davis, *RES*, XIV (1963), 415–417; D. P. French, *BA*,
   XXXVII (1963), 160–163; M. J. C. Hodgart, *Essays in Criti-
   cism*, XIII (1963), 274–277; G. Mayhew, *SAQ*, LXII (1963),
   311–313; V. Mercier, *HR*, XVI (1963), 290–296; E. Pons,
   EA, XVI (1963), 84–86; I. Simon, *Revue des Langues Vi-
   vantes*, XXIX (1963), 146–152; E. Rosenheim, *MP*, LXII
   (1964), 75–81. Also, see Johnston (109).

Elliott, Robert C. "Swift's 'Little' Harrison, Poet and Continua-   [87]
   tor of the *Tatler*," *SP*, XLVI (1949), 544–559.
   More about Harrison than Swift. See Swift's account of
   Harrison in the *Journal to Stella*.

Fisher, J. J., Jr. "Dean Swift as a Human Being; Reply," *At-*   [88]
   lantic Monthly, December 1950, p. 22.
   A reply to Gogarty (93). See Johnston (109), Morrall
   (121), Pons and Axelrad (132).

FitzGerald, Brian. *The Anglo-Irish, Three Representative*   [89]
   Types: Cork, Ormonde, Swift. London, 1952.
   Reviewed by *TLS*, December 12, 1952, p. 816; P. Hinkson,
   Fortnightly, (1952), No. 1032, pp. 425–426.

Foote, Michael. *The Pen and the Sword.* London, 1957.   [90]
A popular account of Swift and Marlborough.

Gabel, Joseph. "Swift et la schizophrénic. Le point de vue du   [91]
psychiatre," *Psyché*, IV (1949), 253–258.
Argues for a relationship.

Gimblett, C. "The Great Dean and the Young Preacher,"   [92]
LQ&HR, CLXX (1945), 160–162.
See Barnds (64), Bennett (66), Landa (114), White (148),
and Beckett (171).

Gogarty, Oliver St. John. "Dean Swift As a Human Being,"   [93]
Atlantic Monthly, October 1950, pp. 54–56.
Revives the discredited notion that Swift and Stella were
the illegitimate children of John and William Temple. See
Johnston (109), Morrall (121), Pons and Axelrad (132), and
particularly Fisher (88).

Goldgar, Bertrand A. *The Curse of Party: Swift's Relations with*   [94]
Addison and Steele. Lincoln, Nebraska, 1961.
Reviewed by D. J. Greene, *PQ*, XLI (1962), 629–630; W.
B. Coley, *CE*, XXIII (1962), 513; R. Paulson, *JEGP*, XLI
(1962), 648–650; D. P. French, *BA*, XXXVII (1963), 160–163.
See Hopkins (101).

Greenacre, Phyllis. *Swift and Carroll: A Psychoanalytic Study*   [95]
of Two Lives. New York, 1955.
Reviewed by I. Ehrenpreis, *PQ*, XXXV (1956), 330–332.
See Greenacre (96).

———. "The Mutual Adventures of Jonathan Swift and Lemuel   [96]
Gulliver," *Psychoanalytic Quarterly*, XXIV (1955), 60.
See Greenacre (95).

Hall, F. G. *History of the Bank of Ireland.* Dublin and Oxford,   [97]
1949.
Swift is treated briefly in Chapter I.

Hallett, Paul H. "From Swift to Inge," *Priest*, X (April 1954),　　[98]
316–321.

Hardy, Evelyn. *The Conjured Spirit—Swift: A Study in the Re-*　　[99]
lationship of Swift, Stella, and Vanessa. London, 1949.
　　Reviewed by *TLS*, December 9, 1949, p. 811; also Clifford
(192). See Ehrenpreis (83) and (84), Le Brocquy (115), and
Yost (162).

Henchy, Patrick. "Irish History in Irish Engravings," *Antiques*,　[100]
LVII (March 1950), 182–185.
　　A reproduction of a portrait of Swift by Andrew Miller.

Hopkins, Robert H. "The Issue of Anonymity and the Begin-　[101]
ning of the Steele-Swift Controversy of 1713–14: A New
Interpretation," *ELN*, II (1964), 15–21.
　　Contends that scholars should no longer feel compelled to
use ethical values to defend Steele and only aesthetic values
to defend Swift. Steele is more of an opportunist who plotted
a course of action that succeeded admirably after the death of
Queen Anne. Concludes: "if Swift was the superior artist,
Steele was the superior politician." See Goldgar (94).

Jackson, R. Wyse. "Stella's Signatures," *TLS*, December 29,　[102]
1945, p. 624.
　　On Dublin title deeds. See Ehrenpreis (82) and O'Leary
(131).

———. *Swift and His Circle: A Book of Essays*. Dublin, 1945.　[103]
　　Included are Mrs. Barber, Mrs. Whiteway, Mrs. Pilkington,
and others.

Jacobs, Monty. *Jonathan Swift*. Berlin, 1948.　　　　　　　[104]
　　A popular biography intended for German readers.

Jaggard, William. " 'The Cheshire Sheaf': Swift's Lodging in [105]
Chester," *N&Q*, CXC (1946), 18.
On three epigrams written at Chester by Swift.

John Oldmixon, Reflections on Dr. Swift's Letter to Harley [106]
(1712); and Arthur Mainwaring, The British Academy
(1712). Augustan Reprint Society, 1948.

Johnson, Maurice. "A Literary Chestnut: Dryden's 'Cousin [107]
Swift'," *PMLA*, LXVII (1952), 1024–1034.
See Moore and Johnson (120), Mundy (122).

——. "Swift and 'The Greatest Epitaph in History'," *PMLA*, [108]
LXVIII (1953), 814–827.
Assumes that Swift's epitaph is a conscious work of art
composed from the material of his experience.

Johnston, Denis. *In Search of Swift*. Dublin, London, and New [109]
York, 1959.
Reviewed by D. Davie, *New Statesman*, LVIII (1959), 549;
F. Kermode, *Spectator*, November 6, 1959, p. 639; L. Landa,
PQ, XXXIX (1960), 361–363; F. Brady, *YR*, XLIX (1960),
598–602; J. C. Beckett, *Irish Historical Studies*, XII (1960),
165–167; P. Cruttwell, *HR*, XIII (1960), 441; H. Davis, *RES*,
XII (1961), 208–210. See Ehrenpreis (86), Fisher (88), Go-
garty (93), Le Brocquy (115), Morrall (121), Pons and Axel-
rad (132).

——. "Trouble with Swift," *Nation*, CXCVI (January 26, [110]
1963), 73–76.
A review-article. See Ehrenpreis (86), Ferguson (444), and
Le Brocquy (115).

Landa, Louis A. "The Critical Significance of Biographical Evi-   [111]
dence: Swift," in *English Institute Essays*, 1946. New York,
1947, pp. 20–40.

———. "Swift's Deanery Income: A New Document," in *Pope*   [112]
and His Contemporaries: Essays Presented to George Sher-
burn (Edited by James L. Clifford and Louis A. Landa). Oxford, 1949, pp. 159–170.
   Discusses all the documents concerning the deanery income
and concludes: "On the whole, then, Swift deserves no great
sympathy when he cries out his financial woes."

———. "The Insolent Rudeness of Dr. Swift," *MLN*, LXVIII   [113]
(1953), 223–226.
   Concerns Swift's quarrel with John Evans, Bishop of
Meath.

———. *Swift and the Church of Ireland*. Oxford, 1954.   [114]
   Reviewed by *TLS*, December 17, 1954, p. 823; H. Williams,
PQ, XXXIV (1955), 319–321; J. C. Beckett, *Irish Historical*
Studies, IX (1955), 350–351; D. Donoghue, *Studies*, XLIV
(1955), 499; I. Ehrenpreis, *JEGP*, LIV (1955), 422–424; R.
Kirk, *Historical Magazine of the Protestant Episcopal Church*,
XXIV (1955), 214–215; J. F. Maclear, *Journal of Religion*,
XXXV (1955), 259–260; P. V. Norwood, *Church History*,
XXIV (1955), 376–377; M. J. Quinlan, *Review of Religion*,
XX (1955), 68–70; C. Peake, *MLR*, L (1955), 568–569; C. J.
Stranks, *Durham University Journal*, XLVII (1955), 84–85;
E. K. Gibson, *MLQ*, XVII (1956), 274; C. J. Horne, *RES*,
VII (1956), 202–205; R. Quintana, *MP*, LIII (1956), 207–208.
See Barnds (64), Bennett (66), Gimblett (92), White (148),
and Beckett (171).

Le Brocquy, Sybil. *Cadenus: A Reassessment in the Light of*   [115]
New Evidence of the Relationships Between Swift, Stella, and
Vanessa. Dublin, 1962.
   Reviewed by G. Bullough, *English*, XIV (1963), 200–202;

E. Pons, *EA*, XVI (1963), 187–188; H. Davis, *RES*, XV
(1964), 91–92; A. Martin, *Studies*, LIII (1964), 211–213. See
Ehrenpreis (83) and (84), Hardy (99), Johnston (110), Mor-
ral (121), Pons and Axelrad (132), Yost (162), Mercier
(268).

Manly, Francis. "Swift Marginalia in Howell's *Medulla His-*   [116]
toriae Anglicanae," *PMLA*, LXXIII (1958), 335–338.
   Swift presented a copy to Mary Harrison with his notes.
The notes reveal a close reading of the work and Swift's char-
acteristic marginal vituperations. See (60), Clarkson (73),
Williams (152).

Marić, Sreten. "Džonatan Svift," *Delo*: Beograd, V (1957),   [117]
880–897.

Mayhew, George P. "Swift's First Will and the First Use of the   [118]
Provost's Negative at T.C.D.," *HLQ*, XXI (1958), 295–322.
   Traces Swift's entire relationship to elections at Trinity
College. The first provost's negative probably was exercised
first in 1727. Discusses the occasion and subsequent uses and
all related documents.

"Moor Park, Surrey, England: Stella's Cottage," *Wilson Li-*   [119]
brary Bulletin, XX (1946), 678–679.
   Photographs with brief notes on their significance to Swift.
See Babcock (62).

Moore, John R., and Maurice Johnson. "Dryden's 'Cousin   [120]
Swift'," *PMLA*, LXVIII (1953), 1232–1240.
   An exchange of opinions. See Johnson (107), Mundy (122).

Morrall, John B. "Around and About Swift," *Studies*, XLIX   [121]
(1960), 305–312.
   See Fisher (88), Gogarty (93), Johnston (109), Le Brocquy
(115), Pons and Axelrad (132).

Mundy, P. D. "The Dryden-Swift Relationship," *N&Q*, [122]
CXCIII (1948), 470–474.
See Johnson (107), Moore and Johnson (120).

——. "The Philpott Family: Ancestors of Jonathan Swift," [123]
N&Q, CXCV (1950), 314–317.
See Mundy (125).

——. "Thomas Swift, 'Brother to Dean Swift'," *N&Q*, CXCV [124]
(1950), 407.
Entry in a parish register.

——. "The Ancestry of Jonathan Swift," *N&Q*, CXCVI [125]
(1951), 381–387.
See Mundy (123).

——. "Jonathan Swift's Chester Relatives," *N&Q*, CXCIX, [126]
N.S. I (1954), 248–249.
Abigail Herrick of Wigston is not Abigail Erick, Swift's
mother. See Mundy (127), Welply (146).

——. "The Mother of Jonathan Swift," *N&Q*, CCIII, N.S. V [127]
(1958), 444–445.
Discusses the known facts and apparent difficulties in ac-
cepting the two spellings—Abigail Erick or Herrick. See
Mundy (126).

Murry, John Middleton. *Jonathan Swift: A Critical Biography*. [128]
London, 1954.
Reviewed by *TLS*, April 16, 1954, p. 248; I. Ehrenpreis,
PQ, XXXIV (1955), 322–323; J. C. Beckett, *Irish Historical
Studies*, IX (1955), 349–350; H. Davis, *RES*, VI (1955),
319–321; D. Donoghue, *Studies*, XLIV (1955), 119–121; *YR*,
XLV (1956), viii–x. See Clifford (193).

——. *Swift*. London, 1955. [129]
A pamphlet intended to serve as an introduction to Swift
and his writings.

O'Hegarty, P. S. "Jonathan Swift: Irishman," *Bell*, X (1945), [130]
478–483.

O'Leary, J. J. "Swift and Esther," *TLS*, November 27, 1953, [131]
p. 761.
Notes the purchase of Talbot's Castle in Trim, County
Meath by Stella, Feb. 6, 1717, and her sale of it to Swift, May
10, 1718. See Ehrenpreis (82) and Jackson (102).

Pons, Emile, and José Axelrad. "Rénovation de la Biographie [132]
Swiftienne?" *EA*, XIV (1961), 314–320.
See Fisher (88), Gogarty (93), Johnston (109), Le Brocquy
(115), and Morrall (121).

Rogers, Katherine M. "Jonathan Swift's Attitude Toward [133]
Women," Unpublished dissertation, Columbia University,
1957.
See *DA*, XVII (1957), 1767–1768. Also, see Rogers (134).

———. " 'My Female Friends': the Misogyny of Jonathan Swift," [134]
TSLL, I (1959), 366–379.
Contends that Swift's misogyny is evident in his writings.
See Rogers (133).

Romm, A. "Preobraženie Džonatana Svifta," *Voprosy Litera-* [135]
tury, VII (1963), 149–159.

Rowse, A. L. "Swift at Letcombe," in *The English Past*, New [136]
York, 1951, pp. 113–142.
Discusses his residence at Letcombe and the writing of
Free Thoughts on the Present State of Affairs.

Slepian, Barry. "Jonathan Swift and George Faulkner," Unpub- [137]
lished dissertation, University of Pennsylvania, 1962.
See *DA*, XXIII (1962), 1689.

———. "When Swift First Employed George Faulkner," *PBSA*, [138]
LVI (1962), 354–356.
Between October 1729 and May 1730. The edition of "A

Vindication of . . . Lord Carteret," published in April 1730, was probably the first work Swift employed Faulkner to print.

————. "Some Forgotten Anecdotes About Swift," *Bulletin of*   [139]
the New York Public Library, LXVIII (1964), 33–44.
Concerns the text of Faulkner's "Further Account" from his octavo edition of Volume XI of Swift's *Works* (1762). Indicates its value as contemporary biography.

Snethlage, Jacob L. *Jonathan Swift, de Englese Voltaire*. Den   [140]
Haag, 1962.

Subramanyam, N. S. *Jonathan Swift*. Masters of English Lit-   [141]
erature Series, Number 2. Allahabad, 1962.

Sun, Phillip Su Yue. "Swift's Eighteenth-Century Biographies,"   [142]
Unpublished dissertation, Yale University, 1963.
See Williams (153).

Teerink, Herman. "Swift's Ordination, 1694–5," *Dublin Maga-*   [143]
zine, XXII (1947), 7–9.

————. "Swifte of Rotherham," *N&Q*, CXCV (1950), 41–42.   [144]
Lists genealogies and mentions persons yet unidentified.

"The Melancholy of Swift," *TLS*, October 20, 1945, p. 498.   [145]
Finds Swift expressing his discontentment with human life in utterances approaching the "dark sublime."

Welply, W. H. "Jonathan Swift's Chester Relatives," *N&Q*,   [146]
CXCIX, N.S. I (1954), 339–340.
See Mundy (126).

————. "Swift's Grandfather," *TLS*, July 17, 1959, p. 423.   [147]
See Ehrenpreis (85).

White, Newport B. (Editor). *The "Dignitas Decani" of St.* [148]
Patrick's Cathedral, Dublin. Dublin, 1957.
  See Barnds (64), Bennett (66), Gimblett (92), Landa
(114), Beckett (171).

Wiley, A. N. "A Probable Source of the Text of Sheridan's 'In- [149]
ventory' As Printed in the *Cheltenham Journal*," *N&Q*,
CXCIII (1948), 186–187.
  The third printing of Sheridan's verses, an eighteenth-
century version made for J. Almon, the political pamphleteer.
Included in *The Fugitive Miscellany*, London, 1774, pp. 125–
126. See Wiley (150).

——. "Un-recorded Printings of Thomas Sheridan's 'Inventory' [150]
of Dean Swift's Goods at Laracor," *N&Q*, CXCIII (1948),
56–57. (Addendum, pp. 186–187).
  See Wiley (149).

Williams, Sir Harold. "Old Mr. Lewis," *RES*, XXI (1945), [151]
56–57.
  In his *Life of Swift* Samuel Johnson refers to a conversation
between the Earl of Orrery and old Mr. Lewis, and he draws
a mistaken conclusion regarding Swift's writing *The History
of the Last Four Years of the Queen*. Erasmus Lewis is the
man in question.

——. "Swift and Shakespeare," *N&Q*, CXCIII (1948), 194–195. [152]
  Concerns Swift's library. See (60), Clarkson (73), and
Manly (116).

——. "Swift's Early Biographers," in *Pope and His Contempo-* [153]
raries: Essays Presented to George Sherburn (Edited by James
L. Clifford and Louis A. Landa). Oxford, 1949, pp. 114–128.
  Discusses Swift's fragmentary autobiography, five publica-
tions by people who had known him, Sheridan, and Johnson.
See Sun (142).

Wilson, T. G. "A Hitherto Undescribed Death-Mask of Dean   [154]
Swift," *Journal of the Royal Society of Antiquaries of Ireland*, LXXXI (1951), 107–114.
    See Wilson (155), (157), (159).

——. "The Death Masks of Dean Swift," *Princeton Univer-*   [155]
sity Library Chronicle, XVI (1955), 107–110.
    See Wilson (154), (157), (159).

——. "The Mental and Physical Health of Dean Swift," *Medi-*   [156]
cal History, II (1958), 175–190.
    Reviewed by L. Landa, *PQ*, XXXVIII (1959), 358: "noth-
ing new or valuable." See Brain (68).

——. "The Death-Masks of Swift," *Medical History*, IV   [157]
(1960), 49–58.
    See Wilson (154), (155), (159).

——. "Swift's Personality," *REL*, III (1962), 39–58.   [158]
    See Ehrenpreis (84).

——. "Swift's Death-Masks," *REL*, III (1962), 58–68.   [159]
    See Wilson (154), (155), (157).

——. "Swift and the Doctors," *Medical History*, VIII (1964),   [160]
199–216.
    See Brain (68), Ehrenpreis (84).

Woolley, David. "A Reference to Swift," *Johnsonian News*   [161]
Letter, XIII (1953), No. 4, 2–3.
    In White Kennett's diary.

Yost, George, Jr. "Well-filled Silences: the Case of Swift and   [162]
Vanessa," *Florida State University Studies*, XI (1953), 25–55.
    See Ehrenpreis (83) and (84), Hardy (99), Le Brocquy
(115).

    See (171), (172), (173), (174), (185), (204), (217), (218),
(230), (235), (239), (245), (255), (261), (262), (265), (269),
(273), (281), (294), (296), (299), (309), (315), (316), (323),
(328), (334), (335), (345), (425), (461), (463), (465), (468),
(532).

III

General Criticism

"A Note on Samuel Butler (1612–1680) and Jonathan Swift," [163]
N&Q, CCIII, N.S. V (1958), 294–296.
Parallels suggest that Swift may have seen Butler's manuscripts.

Alexander, Jean. "Yeats and the Rhetoric of Defilement," *REL*, [164]
VI (1965), 44–57.
Comparisons and contrasts with Swift's work. In Swift the
images of defilement are intended to obliterate beauty and
eroticism by making the reader recoil from the object which
has gross animal functions. See Torchiana (327).

Atherton, James S. *The Books at the Wake: A Study of Literary* [165]
Allusions in James Joyce's "Finnegan's Wake." New York,
1960.
Allusions to Swift in *Finnegan's Wake*. See Atherton (166),
Jarrell (242).

———. "A Few More Books at the Wake," *James Joyce Quar-* [166]
terly, II (1964), 142–149.
See Atherton (165), Jarrell (242).

Atkins, John William Hey. "Neo-classicism Challenged: Den- [167]
nis, Addison, Pope, Swift, Welsted, and Blackwell," in *English*

Literary Criticism: Seventeenth and Eighteenth Centuries.
London, 1951, pp. 173–176.
Discusses Swift's views on contemporary criticism as part
of his campaign against dullness and pedantry.

Barzun, Jacques. "Swift or Man's Capacity for Reason," in *The*   [168]
Energies of Art, New York, 1956, pp. 81–100.
Concerns Swift's satiric strategy. See Kelling (250).

Beaumont, Charles A. *Swift's Classical Rhetoric.* (University of   [169]
Georgia Monographs, No. 8). Athens, Georgia, 1961.
Reviewed by D. C. Bryant, *PQ*, XLI (1962), 628; R. Paul-
son, *JEGP*, LXI (1962), 649–650; R. S. Pomeroy, *Quarterly
Journal of Speech*, XLVIII (1962), 322–323; R. Quintana,
Georgia Review, XVII (1963), 95–97; K. Williams, *RES*,
XIV (1963), 324–325.

——. *Swift's Use of the Bible: A Documentation and a Study*   [170]
in Allusion. Athens, Georgia, 1965.

Beckett, J. C. "Swift As an Ecclesiastical Statesman," in *Essays*   [171]
in British and Irish History in Honor of James Eadie Todd
(Edited by H. A. Cronne, T. W. Moody and D. B. Quinn).
London, 1949, pp. 135–152.
See Barnds (64), Bennett (66), Gimblett (92), Landa
(114), White (148).

Béranger, J. "Swift en 1714: Position Politique et Sentiments   [172]
Personnels," *EA*, XV (1962), 233–247.
Concerns the effect of Queen Anne's death on Swift's
career.

Brady, Frank. "The Terrible Encounter; Jonathan Swift and   [173]
the Human Race," *YR*, LII (1963), 267–270.
Review-article. See Ehrenpreis (86).

Bredvold, Louis I. "The Gloom of the Tory Satirists," in *Pope* [174] *and His Contemporaries: Essays Presented to George Sherburn* (Edited by James L. Clifford and Louis A. Landa). Oxford, 1949, pp. 1–19.

———. "The Tory Satirists: Jonathan Swift," in *The Literature* [175] *of the Restoration and the Eighteenth Century, 1660–1798,* Vol. III of *A History of English Literature* (Edited by Hardin Craig). New York, 1962, pp. 67–76.

Brengle, R. L. "Very Knowing Americans. Jonathan Swift and [176] America: His Reputation and Influence, 1720-1860," Unpublished dissertation, Columbia University, 1961.
See *DA*, XXIII (1962), 1682–1683.

Briggs, H. E. "Swift and Keats," *PMLA*, LXI (1946), 1101– [177] 1108.
Keats refers to Swift in several of his letters, imitates his style on occasion, and incorporates reminiscences of Swift's work in at least five of his poems.

Brown, James. "Swift as Moralist," *PQ*, XXXIII (1954), 368– [178] 387.
Reviewed by E. Tuveson, *PQ*, XXXIV (1955), 315–317. See R. M. Frye (535).

Brown, Norman O. "The Excremental Vision," in *Life Against* [179] *Death: The Psychoanalytical Meaning of History*. Middletown, Conn., 1959.
Principally a consideration of the poems and *Gulliver*.

Bullitt, John M. *Jonathan Swift and the Anatomy of Satire: A* [180] *Study of Satiric Technique*. Cambridge, Mass., 1953.
Reviews: *TLS*, August 28, 1953, p. 547; I. Ehrenpreis, *PQ*, XXXIII (1954), 300–301; R. C. Elliott, *MLN*, LXIX (1954), 518–521; C. J. Horne, *RES*, V (1954), 420–423; N. Knox,

SAQ, LIII (1954), 158–159; R. Quintana, *JEGP*, LIII (1954), 114–117; C. Tracy, *QQ*, LXI (1954), 282–284; J. R. Sutherland, *MLR*, L (1955), 331–332. See Clifford (193).

Burgess, C. F. "The Genius of *The Beggar's Opera*," *Cithera*,   [181] II (1962), 6–12.
Too much has been made of Gay's dependence on Swift, Pope, and Arbuthnot. "Similitude of manners in high and low life" preoccupied Gay *before* Swift's suggestion of a "Newgate pastoral."

Butt, John E. "Swift," in *The Augustan Age*. London, 1950,   [182] pp. 46–60.
A general discussion showing that Swift considered the triumphs of reason to be illusory.

Buxton, George. "Swift et sa Satire Universelle," *Revue de*   [183] *l'Universite d'Ottawa*, XIX (July 1949), 379–390.

Canseliet, Eugène. "L'Hermétisme dans la Vie de Swift et dans   [184] ses 'Voyages'," *Cashiers du Sud*, XLVI (1958), 15–30.
Claims that hermetical and alchemical significances are discoverable in many of Swift's words and ideas; e.g., *Stella* refers to the ruling star of the Hermeticists, to Sophia, wisdom, the virgin of the alchemists.

Carroll, John. "Richardson on Pope and Swift," *UTQ*, XXXIII   [185] (1963), 19–29.
Richardson's objections to Swift: "his wit was arrogant, his imagination corrupt, and his writings a libel on human nature." Nor did he heal with morals what he hurt with wit.

Churchill, R. C. *He Served Human Liberty: An Essay on the*   [186] *Genius of Jonathan Swift*. London, 1946.
An uncritical account of Swift's achievements.

Clark, J. Kent. "Swift and the Aristocracy," *Abstracts of Dis-* [187]
sertations, Stanford University, 1949–1950, XXV (1950),
127–128.

———. "Swift and the Dutch," *HLQ,* XVII (1954), 345–356. [188]
Argues that Swift's hatred of the Dutch is related to his religious and political convictions and his interpretation of the
historical events of the time. See Leyburn (256) and Brown
(500).

Clark, Paul O. "Swift's Little Language and Nonsense Names," [189]
JEGP, LVI (1957), 154–157.
See Smith (317).

Clayborough, Arthur. *The Grotesque in English Literature.* [190]
Oxford, 1965, pp. 112–157.
Concerns Swift's intellectual attitude and his use of fantasy
and logic.

Clifford, James L. "Works on Swift," *Johnsonian News Letter,* [191]
X (1950), No. 5, 4–6.
See Johnson (359) and Starkman (420).

———. "Swift Studies," *Johnsonian News Letter,* XI (1951), No. [192]
3, 10.
See Hardy (99).

———. "Recent Books on Swift," *Johnsonian News Letter,* XIV [193]
(1954), No. 2, 1–3.
See Bullitt (180), Ewald (215), Murry (128), and Price
(289).

———. "The Eighteenth Century," *MLQ,* XXVI (1965), 111– [194]
134.
On recent scholarship.

Connolly, Cyril. "Sterne and Swift," *Atlantic Monthly*, June   [195]
1945, pp. 94–96.

Cook, Richard I. "Swift's Polemical Characters," *Discourse*, VI   [196]
(1962–1963), 30–38 and 43–48.
Swift used the Theophrastan character to attack specific
men. Even describing a "good" character, Swift's praise is
ironic in terms of mock-criticism; his pose of detachment in
the histories is less successful in praise than in attack.

Davidson, J. A. "Bentley and the Greeks," *Proceedings of the*   [197]
Leeds Philosophical and Literary Society, X (1963), 117–127.
Defends Bentley against attacks on him by Swift and Pope.
See Maguinness (264).

Davie, Donald. "Academism and Jonathan Swift," *Twentieth*   [198]
Century, CLIV (1953), 217–224.
On the methods of Bullitt and Quintana.

Davis, Herbert. "The Conciseness of Swift," in *Essays on the*   [199]
Eighteenth Century Presented to David Nichol Smith in
Honor of his Seventieth Birthday. Oxford, 1945, pp. 15–32.
Formulates a theory about Swift's style and concerns him-
self with style as internal evidence in matters of canon. See
Fussell (11).

⸺. *The Satire of Jonathan Swift*. New York, 1947.   [200]
Reviewed by I. Ehrenpreis, *PQ*, XXVIII (1949), 404–405;
A. N. Jeffares, *English Studies*, XXIX (1948), 22–24; R.
Quintana, *MLN*, LXIII (1948), 578.

⸺. "The Conversation of the Augustans," in *The Seventeenth*   [201]
Century: Studies in the History of Thought and Literature
from Bacon to Pope, by Richard Foster Jones and Others
Writing in His Honor. Stanford, 1951, pp. 181–197.

⸺. "Recent Studies of Swift and Johnson," in *Sprache und*   [202]
Literatur Englands und Amerikas. Dritter Band: *Die Wissen-*

schaftliche Erschliessung der Prosa (Hrsg. von Gerhard Muller-Schwefe in Gemeinschaft mit Hermann Metzger). Tubingen, 1959, pp. 534–535.

———. "The Augustan Conception of History," in *Reason and*   [203] *the Imagination: Studies in the History of Ideas, 1600–1800* (Edited by J. A. Mazzeo). New York and London, 1962, pp. 213–229.

● ———. *Jonathan Swift, Essays on His Satire and Other Studies.*   [204] New York, 1964.
   Previously published essays.

◕ Dennis, Nigel. "On Swift and Satire," *Encounter*, XXII (1964),   [205] No. 3, 14–28.
   What Swift satirized was present in himself; he unites moral authority and abnormal violence.

Dobrée, Bonamy. *English Literature in the Early Eighteenth*   [206] *Century, 1700–1740.* New York and London, 1959, pp. 54–73, 84–102, 432–475, 681–688.

Durant, Jack D. "The Imagery in Swift's Prose: A Descriptive   [207] Analysis of Forms and Functions," Unpublished dissertation, University of Tennessee, 1963.
   See *DA*, XXIV (1964), 4577–4578.

• Dyson, A. E. "Swift: The Metamorphosis of Irony," *Essays and*   [208] *Studies*, N.S. XI (1958), 53–67.
   Swift's irony "ceases to be a functional technique serving a moral purpose and becomes an embodiment of an attitude to life"; it "transmutes itself into a savage exploration of the world's essential immendability."

Ehrenpreis, Irvin. "Swift on Liberty," *JHI*, XIII (1952), 131–   [209] 146.
   Swift "exhibits those neo-classical traits made familiar by

A. O. Lovejoy as uninformitarianism, rationalistic anti-intellectualism, and a negative philosophy of history. . . ."
See Torchiana (327).

———. "Swift and Satire," *CE*, XIII (1952), 309–312.   [210]
His simple irony is plain enough, but he can be ironic about
an irony. At times he uses "triple irony"; at other times, "suppressed irony." His use of *personae* encourages the ordinary
reader to identify with the protagonist.

———. "Four of Swift's Sources," *MLN*, LXX (1955), 95–100.   [211]
In *The Battle of the Books*, "A Description of a City
Shower," and Book III of *Gulliver's Travels*. The sources include passages from Marvell's *Rehearsal Transpos'd*, Blackmore's *King Arthur* and Dryden's translation of the *Aeneid*.

———."Personae," in *Restoration and Eighteenth Century Literature: Essays in Honor of Alan Dugald McKillop* (Edited   [212]
by Carroll Camden). Chicago, 1963, pp. 25–37.
Finds the application of this device to be generally misleading.

Elliott, Robert C. "Swift and Dr. Eachard," *PMLA*, LXIX   [213]
(1954), 1250–1257.
Points to significant parallels.

Elsoffer-Kamins, Louise. "Un Imitateur Original de Jonathan   [214]
Swift: l'Abbé Coyer et ses *Bagatelles Morales (1754)*," *Revue
de Littérature Comparée*, XXIII (1949), 469–481.

Ewald, William B., Jr. *The Masks of Jonathan Swift*. Cam-   [215]
bridge, Mass., 1954.
Reviewed by M. Mack, *PQ*, XXXIV (1955), 318–319; I.
Ehrenpreis, *MP*, LIII (1955), 134–136; O. W. Ferguson,
JEGP, LIV (1955), 141–142; C. Peake, *MLR*, L (1955), 569;

H. Williams, *RES*, VI (1955), 206–207; H. Kelling, *MLN*, LXXI (1956), 129–131. See Clifford (193).

Falle, George. "Swift's Writings and a Variety of Commenta- [216] tors," *UTQ*, XXXIV (1965), 294–312.
Review-article.

Ferguson, Oliver W. "Jonathan Swift, Freeman of Dublin," [217] *MLN*, LXXI (1956), 405–409.
In 1730 Swift received a gold box as a freeman of the city from the Dublin Corporation, the most tangible reward he was ever to have for his services on behalf of Ireland.

Fiore, Jordan D. "Jonathan Swift and the American Episco- [218] pate," *WMQ*, XI (1954), 425–433.
Describes Swift's "one interest in American activities"; the Anglican episcopate in the American mainland colonies never became a reality.

Fletcher, John. "Samuel Beckett et Jonathan Swift: Vers une [219] Etude Comparée," *Littératures*, X (1962), 81–117.

Fluchère, Henri. *Laurence Sterne de l'homme à l'oeuvre: Biog-* [220] *raphie critique et essai d'interprétation de Tristram Shandy*. Paris, 1961.
References to Swift.

French, David P. "Swift, the Non-Jurors, and Jacobitism," [221] *MLN*, LXXII (1957), 258–264.
Finds that in the early nineties, "Swift was half tempted to accept the non-juring position, and he shows more than a tinge of Jacobitism."

———. "Swift and Hobbes—A Neglected Parallel," *Boston Uni-* [222] *versity Studies in English*, III (1957), 243–255.
Both "write on the assumption that men are motivated by

selfishness; both assume that government is as absolute as force can render it; both define law in terms of compulsion; and both state categorically that men should follow the government religion even, if necessary, at the expense of a hypocritical split between inward belief and outward conformity."

———. "Recent Books About Jonathan Swift," *BA*, XXXVII   [223]
(1963), 160–163.
    See Ehrenpreis (86), Goldgar (94).

Frost, William. "Recent Studies in the Restoration and Eigh-   [224]
teenth Century," *SEL*, II (1962), 359–384.
    See also Greene (228), Halsband (231), Price (291), Spacks (318).

Fussell, Paul, Jr. *The Rhetorical World of Augustan Humanism:*   [224a]
Ethics and Imagery from Swift to Burke. Oxford, 1965.
    Treats Swift rather fully in terms of his ethical position.

Galey, Matthieu. "Une Vie de 'Yahoo'," *Revue de Paris*, LXXI   [225]
(1964), 116–122.
    A review-article equating Swift and Gulliver.

Gilbert, Jack G. "Knaves, Fools, and Heroes: Jonathan Swift's   [226]
Ethics," Unpublished dissertation, University of Texas, 1962.
    See *DA*, XXIII (1962), 1700.

Gilmore, T. B., Jr., "The Reaction to Satire in England from   [227]
1693 to 1761," Unpublished dissertation, University of Illinois, 1964.
    See *DA*, XXV (1965), 1192. Deals mainly with Pope and Swift.

Goldgar, Bertrand A. "Satires on Man and 'The Dignity of   [227a]
Human Nature'," *PMLA*, LXXX (1965), 535–541.
    Concerns critical attacks on satires written by Swift, Gay, Mandeville, and others.

Greene, D. J. "Recent Studies in the Restoration and Eighteenth [228]
Century," *SEL*, I (1961), 115–141.
See also Frost (224), Halsband (231), Price (291), Spacks
(318).

Gros, Léon-Gabriel. "Avant-Propos," in "Langues Imaginaires [229]
et Langage Secret chez Swift," *Cashiers du Sud*, XLVI
(1958), 3–4.
The systematic character of Swift's imaginary languages is
consistent with his skepticism, rationalism, and cynicism.

Guidi, Augusto. "Swift pessimista," *Rassegna d'Italia*, II, (1947), [230]
57–60.

Halsband, Robert. "Recent Studies in the Restoration and Eigh- [231]
teenth Century," *SEL*, III (1963), 433–447.
See also Frost (224), Greene (228), Price (291), Spacks
(318).

Hawkins, Sherman H. "Swift's Physical Imagery: The Medical [232]
Background and the Theological Tradition," Unpublished
dissertation, Princeton University, 1960.
See *DA*, XXI (1961), 3451.

Herrde, Dietrich. *Die Satire als Form der Gesellschaftskritik- [233]
dargestellt am Werke Jonathan Swifts*. Leipzig, 1955.

Highet, Gilbert. *The Anatomy of Satire*. Princeton, N.J., 1962. [234]
Commentaries on many of Swift's writings.

Hogan, J. J. "Bicentenary of Jonathan Swift, 1667–1745," [235]
Studies, XXXIV (1945), 501–510.

Holloway, John. "The Well-filled Dish: An Analysis of [236]
Swift's Satire," *HR*, IX (1956), 20–37.
Discusses Swift's satire in terms of how "its satirical indictment is created; and how much, in this or that given
case, the indictment contains."

● Honig, Edwin. "Notes on Satire in Swift and Jonson," *New* [237]
Mexico Quarterly Review, XVIII (1948), 155–163.
Jonson and Swift construct a situation which challenges
the reader's most warmly pledged ideologies and beliefs. In
Swift the effect is that of looking at ourselves in a distorted
mirror; in Jonson the effect is like the one which provokes
the spontaneous laugh in our response to the "dirty joke."

———. *Dark Conceit: The Making of Allegory*. Evanston, Ill., [238]
1959.
Compares Swift's satire, principally in *Gulliver*, and the
uses of allegory; sees external deformity in Swift as representing moral deformity.

Honoré, Jean. "Charles Gildon rédacteur du *British Mercury* [239]
(1711–1712): les attaques contre Pope, Swift, et les Wits,"
EA, XV (1962), 347–364.

Hori, Daiji. *Swift and Others*. Tokyo, 1959. [240]

Huebner, Wayne. "Convention and Innovation in the Satirical [241]
Treatment of Women by the Major Satirists of the Early
Eighteenth Century," Unpublished dissertation, University
of Minnesota, 1964.
See *DA*, XXV (1964), 2961.

Jarrell, Mackie L. "Swiftiana in *Finnegan's Wake*," *ELH*, [242]
XXVI (1959), 271–294.
See Atherton (165) and (166).

———. "'Jack and the Dane': Swift Traditions in Ireland," [243]
Journal of American Folklore, LXXVII (1964), 99–117.
Concerns Swift's relation to the oral tradition as recorded
by the Irish Folklore Commission.

Jefferson, D. W. "An Approach to Swift," in *The Pelican* [244]
Guide to English Literature (Edited by Boris Ford). Vol. 4.
Baltimore, 1957, 230–250.
An excellent introductory essay to Swift's writings.

Jensen, Johannes V. *Swift og Oehlenschläger.* Copenhagen, [245]
1950.
   Three essays on Swift. See *TLS*, January 26, 1951, p. 52.

Johnson, James W. "Scythia, Cato, and Corruption: Swift's His- [246]
torical Concepts and Their Background," Unpublished dissertation, Vanderbilt University, 1954.
   See *DA*, XIV (1954), 1396–1397. Also see Johnson (247)
and Rosenbaum (302).

——. "Swift's Historical Outlook," *Journal of British Studies,* [247]
IV (1965), 52–77.
   See Johnson (246) and Rosenbaum (302).

Johnson, Maurice. "The Ghost of Swift in 'Four Quartets'," [248]
MLN, LXIV (1949), 273.
   The ghost that speaks in Part II of Little Gidding is Swift.

Kassner, Rudolf. *Der Goldene Drachen.* Stuttgart, 1957. [249]
   Includes an essay on Swift.

Kelling, Harold D. "The Appeal to Reason: A Study of Jon- [250]
athan Swift's Critical Theory and Its Relation to His Writings," Unpublished dissertation, Yale University, 1948.
   See Barzun (168).

Kermode, Frank. "Jonathan the First," *New Statesman,* Sep- [251]
tember 14, 1962, pp. 321–322.
   Discusses the effect of what Swift does as depending on
ironical deviation from a norm of common sense, and argues
that he consistently maintains his ironic obliquity.

Kernan, Alvin B. *The Plot of Satire.* New Haven and London, [252]
1965.
   References to many of Swift's works.

Knox, Norman. *The Word "Irony" and Its Context, 1500–*   [253]
1755. Durham, N.C., 1961.
Discusses Swift's ironic stances.

Korninger, Siegfried. *English Literature and Its Background:* [253a]
The Restoration Period and the Eighteenth Century, 1660–
1780. Vienna, 1964.
Swift is treated only in a cursory fashion.

Landa, Louis A. "Swift, the Mysteries, and Deism," in *Studies* [254]
in English, Department of English, the University of Texas,
1944. Austin, 1945, pp. 239–256.
A discussion of Swift's major satires in the light of his sermons. Wary of falling into a thoroughgoing skepticism, Swift
held that "the grand points of Christianity ought to be taken
as infallible revelations."

———. "Jonathan Swift and Charity," *JEGP*, XLIV (1945), [255]
337–350.
Deals with his general views on charitable relief, the stew-
ardship of the wealthy, and the duty of dispensing alms to
the needy. Swift believed in the justice of social hierarchy.

Leyburn, Ellen D. "Swift's View of the Dutch," *PMLA*, LXVI [256]
(1951), 734–745.
Traces the causes of Swift's hostility to that people. See
Clark (188), Brown (500).

———. "Swift's Language Trifles," *HLQ*, XV (1952), 195–200. [257]
Discusses Swift's mock-Latin word games in terms of his
love of mystification and the pleasure he derived from sharing
a secret with the perceptive reader.

Longcore, Chris. "A Possible Echo of Jonathan Swift in Dylan [258]
Thomas," *N&Q*, CCVIII, N.S. V (1963), 153.
In Swift's "An Elegy on . . . Mr. Demar." Swift: "The

Hand that sign'd the mortgage paid the shot." Thomas: "The hand that signed the paper felled a city."

Loomis, C. Grant. "Superstitions and Beliefs in Swift," *Western* [259] *Folklore*, XV (1956), 126–128.
A *Complete Collection of Genteel and Ingenious Conversation* is a folklorist's delight; it lists items with regard to eating and drinking, devil lore, luck, cures, etc.

McCall, Raymond G. "H. L. Mencken and the Glass of Satire," [260] *CE*, XXIII (1962), 633–636.
Suggests that Mencken oversimplified Swift and the eighteenth century for his own purposes.

McDonald, W. U., Jr. "A Letter of Sir Walter Scott to William Scott on the Jeffrey-Swift Controversy," *RES*, XII [261] (1961), 404–408.
Walter praises William for his defense of Swift against Jeffrey's attack.

McElderry, B. R., Jr. "Thackery on Swift and Macaulay on [262] Chatham," *N&Q*, CXCIX, N.S. I (1954), 32.
Macaulay was aided in his characterization of Chatham by his memory of the last sentence of Thackeray's lecture on Swift—the figure of a man resembling an empire falling.

McKillop, A. D. "Jonathan Swift," in *English Literature from* [263] *Dryden to Burns*. New York and London, 1948, pp. 135–146.

Maguinness, W. S. "Bentley as Man and Scholar," *Proceedings* [264] *of the Leeds Philosophical and Literary Society*, X (1963), 93–103.
Argues that Swift's attack on Bentley obscured Bentley's scholarly contributions. See also Davidson (197).

Menon, P. B. K. "Genius and Madness," *Indian Review*, LXI [265]
(1960), 410–412.
Swift, Cowper, de Maupassant, and others bear witness that
genius is related to madness.

Mercier, Vivian. *The Irish Comic Tradition*. Oxford, 1962. [266]
Concerns Swift's influence on Irish writers. See Mercier
(267).

———. "Swift and the Gaelic Tradition," *REL*, III (1962), 69– [267]
79.
Swift's conception of the satirist's role agrees closely with
that held by Gaelic poets from time immemorial, and it in-
fluenced at least two later Gaelic satirists. See Mercier (266).

———. "My Neighbor's Garden, and What I Saw There," *HR*, [268]
XVI (1963), 290–296.
Review-article. See Ehrenpreis (81) and (86), Ferguson
(444) and Le Brocquy (115).

Meyers, Jeffrey. "Swift, Johnson, and the Dublin M.A.," [269]
AN&Q, IV (1965), 5–7.

Milic, Louis T. "A Quantitative Approach to the Style of Jon- [270]
athan Swift," Unpublished dissertation, Columbia University,
1963.
See *DA*, XXIV (1964), 3730.

Moore, John R. "Was Jonathan Swift a Moderate?" *SAQ*, LIII [271]
(1954), 260–267.
Though Swift claimed to be one, "it would not be easy to
justify this from his writings" or from the opinions of his contemporaries.

Neumann, J. H. "Eighteenth-Century Linguistic Tastes as Ex- [272]
hibited in Sheridan's Edition of Swift," *American Speech*,
XXI (1946), 253–263.

Nicolson, Sir Harold George. "Savage Pessimism," in *The Age* [273]
of Reason: The Eighteenth Century. London, 1960, pp. 153–
172.
    A general discussion of Swift and his writings, emphasiz-
ing his frustrated ambitions and political disappointments.
Presents little that has not been said before.

Olson, Robert C. "The Scientific Milieu of Jonathan Swift," [274]
University of Colorado Studies (General Series), XXIX
(1952), 206–209.
    See Owens (276).

Ong, Walter J., S.J. "Swift on the Mind: The Myth of Asep- [275]
sis," *MLQ*, XV (1954), 208–221.
    Examines Swift's conceptualizations and "his way of con-
ceiving psychological operations beyond those of common
sense."

Owens, R. R. "Jonathan Swift's Hostility to Science," Unpub- [276]
lished dissertation, University of Minnesota, 1955.
    See *DA*, XVI (1956), 115–116; also Olson (274).

Pagliaro, Harold E. "Paradox in the Aphorisms of La Roche- [277]
foucauld and Some Representative English Followers,"
PMLA, LXXIX (1964), 42–50.
    Concerns Rochefoucauld's influence upon Swift and others.

Passon, Richard H. "The Satiric Art of Dr. John Arbuthnot," [278]
Unpublished dissertation, University of Notre Dame, 1965.
    See *DA*, XXVI (1966), 5416. Many references to works by
Swift.

———. "Gay to Swift on Political Satire," *AN&Q*, III (1965), 87. [279]
    Gay may have suggested to Swift the idea of satirizing po-
litical pedantry (see *Gulliver*, Book II, Ch. vii) in a letter of
August 16, 1714.

Peake, Charles. "Swift and the Passions," *MLR*, LV (1960),   [280]
169–180.
Swift believed that the passions were the ultimate source
of good and bad in human behavior. Restraint was necessary,
but Swift did not hate the passions as some critics have argued.

Pearson, Hesketh. "Jonathan Swift," in *Lives of the Wits.*   [281]
London, 1962, pp. 1–52.
Obviously intended as an introduction to Swift.

Peterson, Leland D. "The Satiric Norm of Jonathan Swift,"   [282]
Unpublished dissertation, University of Minnesota, 1962.
See *DA*, XXIV (1963), 1605.

Pinkus, Philip. "Satire and St. George," *QQ*, LXX (1963), 30–   [283]
49.
Discusses Swift's relation to satire as the only literary mode
that faces the consequences of evil in this world. See Pinkus
(284).

———. "Sin and Satire in Swift," *BuR*, XIII (1965), 11–25.   [284]
Believes that "Swift's satire arises from a sense of sin and
from the painful awareness of human existence. It does not
cure many vices, or mend many worlds, but by presenting the
image of man's depravity it protests the ways of God to man
with all the passion of his faith." See Pinkus (283).

Pons, Emile. "Swift et Pascal: Note Complementaire," *EA*, IV   [285]
(1952), 319–325.
Finds significant parallels in their philosophical positions.
See Yunck (345).

Preu, James A. "Jonathan Swift and the Common Man," *Flor-*   [286]
ida State University Studies, XI (1953), 19–24.
Concerns Swift's conception of human nature.

———. "Antimonarchism in Swift and Godwin," in *Writers and*   [287]
Their Critics: Studies in English and American Literature

(Florida State University Studies, No. 19). Tallahassee, 1955, pp. 11–28.
  See Preu (288) and (601).

———. *The Dean and the Anarchist*, (Florida State University   [288]
Studies, No. 33). Tallahassee, 1959.
  Swift's influence on Godwin. Reviewed by G. Sherburn,
PQ, XXXIX (1960), 329; also Preu (287) and (601).

Price, Martin. *Swift's Rhetorical Art: A Study in Structure and*   [289]
Meaning. New Haven, 1953.
  Reviewed by I. Ehrenpreis, *PQ*, XXXIII (1954), 300–301;
R. Quintana, *JEGP*, LIII (1954), 114–117; D. Donoghue,
Studies, XLIV (1955), 499–500; E. E. Duncan-Jones, *MLR*, L
(1955), 108; C. J. Horne, *RES*, VI (1955), 204–206; See also
Clifford (193).

———. *To the Palace of Wisdom: Studies in Order and Energy*   [290]
from Dryden to Blake. Garden City, N.Y., 1964, pp. 179–218.
  Contains an excellent chapter on Swift.

———. "Recent Studies in the Restoration and Eighteenth Cen-   [291]
tury," *SEL*, V (1965), 553–574.
  See Frost (224), Greene (228), Halsband (231), and
Spacks (318).

Puhalo, Dušan. "Povodom Priče o buretu i jedne studije o   [292]
Swiftu," *Savremenik*, XI (January 1960), 113–119. [In Yugo-
slavic]

Quintana, Ricardo. "Situational Satire: A Commentary on the   [293]
Method of Swift," *UTQ*, XVII (1948), 130–136.
  See a review by R. J. Allen, *PQ*, XXVIII (1949), 408.

———. *Swift: An Introduction*. London, New York, and To-   [294]
ronto, 1955.
  Reviewed by J. Bullitt, *CE*, XVII (1955), 62–63; D.

Donoghue, *Studies*, XLIV (1955), 121; *TLS*, April 29, 1955, p. 210; M. Clubb, *PQ*, XXXV (1956), 333–334; N. Callan, *MLR*, LI (1956), 246–247; K. Williams, *MLN*, LXXI (1956), 541–544; C. J. Horne, *RES*, VIII (1957), 206–209.

Ravesteyn, W. van. *Satyre als Medicijn: Jonathan Swift*. Arn- [295] hem, 1951.

Redinger, Ruby V. "Jonathan Swift, the Disenchanter," *Amer-* [296] *ican Scholar*, XV (1946), 221–226.
    Finds Swift principally concerned with man's failure to recognize the limitations of his own nature.

Rhodes, Byno R. "Swift and Mandeville As Critics of Society," [297] Unpublished dissertation, Vanderbilt University, 1951.
    See *Bulletin of Vanderbilt University*, LI (1951), 26–27.

Rivers, Charles L. "Swift and Ovid on Hypocrisy," *N&Q*, [298] CXCVI (1951), 496.
    Suggests that Swift's comparison of religion and love in *A Project for the Advancement of Religion* is an allusion to *Ars Amatoria* (Book I, ll. 615–616).

Roberts, Donald R. "A Freudian View of Jonathan Swift," [299] *Literature and Psychology*, VI (1956), 8–17.
    "Unlike the neurotic who dams up his energies within himself, Swift obtained release by sharing his perceptions with the world through art."

Roch, Herbert. *Richter ihrer Zeit: Grimmelshausen, Swift und* [300] *Gogol*. Berlin, 1957.
    Reviewed by M. Colleville, *Etudes Germaniques*, XIII (1958), 365.

Rose, Sister Mary Carmeline, C.S.J. "Problems of Analysis Re- [301] lating to the Fictive Prose of Jonathan Swift," Unpublished dissertation, University of Wisconsin, 1963.
    See *DA*, XXIV (1964), 2895–2896.

Rosenbaum, Morton. "Swift's View of History," *Abstracts of* [302]
Dissertations, University of Wisconsin, XIV (1954), 447–448.
See Johnson (246) and (247).

Rosenheim, Edward W., Jr. *Swift and the Satirist's Art.* Chicago [303]
and London, 1963.
Reviewed by M. Battestin, *CE*, XXV (1963), 162; M. Johnson, *SAQ*, XLII (1963), 612–613; A. Arnold, *Personalist*,
XLV (1964), 124–125; R. Paulson, *JEGP*, LXIII (1964), 169–
176; C. J. Rawson, *N&Q*, CCIX, N.S. XI (1964), 112–113;
C. Robbins, *Journal of Modern History*, XXXVI (1964), 65–
66; J. Sutherland, *PQ*, XLIII (1964), 390–392; J. Traugott,
MLQ, XXV (1964), 205–211; J. R. Wilson, *BA*, XXXVIII
(1964), 311.

Røstvig, Maren-Sofie. *The Background of English Neo-Clas-* [304]
sicism with Some Comments on Swift and Pope. Oslo, 1961.

Rubinstein, Annette T. "Jonathan Swift," in *The Great Tradi-* [305]
tion in English Literature from Shakespeare to Shaw. New
York, 1953, pp. 224–251.
General and superficial.

Sacks, Sheldon. *Fiction and the Shape of Belief: A Study of* [306]
Henry Fielding with Glances at Swift, Johnson and Richard-
son. Berkeley and Los Angeles, 1964.
Gulliver is the principal concern here.

Sams, Henry W. "Swift's Satire of the Second Person," *ELH*, [307]
XXVI (1959), 36–44.
Swift establishes a rhetorical alliance with his readers and
wins their approval and confidence by his attacks on others.
But he sometimes aims his satire at the defenses of his readers
who, unable to bandy it away, must sit down quietly under it.
When this occurs, we have examples of satire in the second
person. See the review by H. Trowbridge, *PQ*, XXXIX
(1960), 364.

Savage, D. S. "Swift," *Western Review*, XV (1950), 25–36.   [308]
A rash, uninformed article that presents nothing new.

Schack, Tage. "Jonathan Swift," in *Afhandlinger*. Copenhagen,   [309]
1947, pp. 139–166.

Scott-Thomas, Lois M. "The Vocabulary of Jonathan Swift,"   [310]
Dalhousie Review, XXV (1946), 442–447.

Scruggs, Charles W. "The Bee and the Spider: Swift's Aesthetic   [311]
and His Role as a Literary Critic," Unpublished dissertation,
University of Wisconsin, 1965.
See *DA*, XXVI (1966), 5417–5418.

Sherburn, George. "Swift," in *A Literary History of England*   [312]
(Edited by A. C. Baugh). New York, 1948.

———. "Gibberish in 1730–1," *N&Q*, CXCVIII (1953), 160–161.   [313]
Pertains to Swift's word-games.

Simons, Mary Lee McCurdy. "A Contribution Toward the   [314]
Study of Jonathan Swift's Sources," Unpublished disserta-
tion, University of Colorado, 1964.
See *DA*, XXV (1965), 5942–5943.

Slepian, Barry. "George Faulkner's *Dublin Journal* and Jonathan   [315]
Swift," *Library Chronicle of the University of Pennsylvania*,
XXXI (1965), 97–116.
A detailed account of their relationship from 1725 until
Swift's last years.

Smidt, Kristian. "Psykologiske Problemar: Swifts liv og Dikt-   [316]
ning," *Edda*, LII (1952), 329–344.

Smith, Roland M. "Swift's Little Language and Nonsense [317]
Names," *JEGP*, LIII (1954), 178–196; and LVI (1957), 157–
162.
Swift may have used Edward Lhuyd's *Archaeologia Britan-
nica* as a source. See Clark (189).

Spacks, Patricia M. "Recent Studies in the Restoration and Eigh- [318]
teenth Century," *SEL*, IV (1964), 497–517.
See also Frost (224), Greene (228), Halsband (231), and
Price (291).

Spector, Ronald D. "Lagerkvist, Swift and the Devices of [319]
Fantasy," *WHR*, XII (1958), 75–79.
Discusses parallels in technique.

Spillane, James M. "Herder and Swift," Unpublished disserta- [320]
tion, Cornell University, 1958.
See *DA*, XIX (1958), 141; Spillane (321) and (322).

———. "Herder's Estimate of Swift," *Kentucky Foreign Lan-* [321]
guage Quarterly, VI (1959), 140–149.
See Spillane (320) and (322).

———. "Herder's Translations from Swift," *Kentucky Foreign* [322]
Language Quarterly, VII (1960), 156–164.
See Spillane (320) and (321).

Stavrou, C. N. "The Love Songs of J. Swift, G. Bernard Shaw [323]
and J. A. A. Joyce," *Midwest Quarterly*, VI (1965), 135–162.
Swift associated marriage with good health and was largely
Pauline in his views on love and marriage.

Sutherland, James. *English Satire*. Cambridge, England, 1958. [324]
Comments briefly on the major satires.

Taylor, Aline M. "Swift's Use of the Term 'Canary Bird'," [325]
MLN, LXXI (1956), 175–177.
Relates Swift's use to a contemporary meaning of the term

—"a rogue or whore taken, and clapp'd into the cage or roundhouse."

Thorpe, Annette P. "Jonathan Swift's Prescription Concerning the English Language," *CLA Journal*, III (1960), 173–180. [326]
　　Finds Swift attacking "corruptions of the language" in a number of works.

Torchiana, Donald T. "W. B. Yeats, Jonathan Swift, and Liberty," *MP*, LXI (1963), 26–39. [327]
　　See Alexander (164) and Ehrenpreis (209).

Traugott, John (Editor). *Discussions of Jonathan Swift*. Boston, 1962. [328]
　　A collection of previously published essays.

——. "The Refractory Swift," *MLQ*, XXV (1964), 205–211. [329]
　　Review-article. See Rosenheim (303).

Trevelyan, G. M. "Jonathan Swift," in *An Autobiography and Other Essays*. London, 1949, pp. 206–210. [330]
　　Finds Swift "supreme as a pamphleteer" but "less successful" as an historian.

Tuveson, Ernest. "Swift and the World Makers," *JHI*, XI (1950), 54–74. [331]
　　Concerns Swift's rejection of the 'modernism' of his times.

—— (Editor). *Swift: A Collection of Critical Essays*. Englewood Cliffs, N.J., 1964. [332]
　　Previously published essays.

Ussher, Arland. "Swift and Mankind," *Dublin Magazine*, XXII (1947), 7–11. [333]

Voigt, Milton. "Swift and Psychoanalytic Criticism," *WHR*, [334]
XVI (1962), 361–367.
An examination of the psychoanalytic studies from
Ferenczi to Ehrenpreis reveals that "whenever art is reduced
to wish-fulfillment . . . we get a mish-mash that is neither
biography nor criticism."

————. *Swift and the Twentieth Century.* Detroit, 1964. [335]
Reviewed by H. Pettit, *ELN*, I (1964), 302–303; C. J.
Rawson, *N&Q*, CCIX, N.S. XI (1964), 314–317; J. Wilson,
BA, XXXVIII (1964), 429; R. Brengle, *PQ*, XLIV (1965),
373–375; J. Stathis, *Comparative Literature Studies*, II (1965),
186–190.

Watt, Ian, and James R. Sutherland. "The Ironic Tradition in [336]
Augustan Prose from Swift to Johnson," in *Restoration and
Augustan Prose* (William Andrews Clark Memorial Li-
brary). Los Angeles, 1956, 19–46.

Weeks, Robert L. "Defoe, Swift, and the Peace of Utrecht," [337]
Unpublished dissertation, University of Indiana, 1956.
See *DA*, XVI (1956), 2171.

Wellek, René. "Studies in Eighteenth-Century Literature," [338]
Erasmus, I (1947), 658–676.
A survey including works on Swift.

West, Paul. "Swift and Dry Religion," *QQ*, LXX (1963), 431– [339]
440.
"Swift turns from man as a soul to man as a social item: he
does not go all the way, but he does tend to deal in ex-
ternals. . . ."

White, H. O. "The Art of Swift," *Hermathena*, LXIX (1947), [340]
1–8.
Extracts from a lecture treating Swift's poetry and his use
of allegory in *A Tale of a Tub* and *Gulliver*. Praises Swift's
prose for its precision and force.

Whittemore, Reed. "But Seriously," *Carleton Miscellany*, III [341]
(1962), 58–76.
Swift is discussed as the ideal, committed satirist.

Williams, Kathleen. *Jonathan Swift and the Age of Compro-* [342]
mise. Lawrence, Kansas, 1958.
Reviewed by E. Tuveson, *PQ*, XXXVIII (1959), 355–
358; J. Butt, *Listener*, LXI (1959), 1077–1078; B. Fabian,
Archiv für das Studium der neueren Sprachen, CXCVI
(1959), 217–218; G. Fraser, *Twentieth Century*, CLXV
(1959), 524–526; W. Ong, *MLQ*, XX (1959), 383–384; R.
Paulson, *JEGP*, LVIII (1959), 297–301; M. Starkman, *His-*
tory of Ideas News Letter, V (1959), 40–42; R. Elliott, *MLN*,
LXXV (1960), 436–439.

——. "Restoration Themes in the Major Satires of Swift," *RES*, [343]
XVI (1965), 258–271.

Worcester, David. *The Art of Satire*. New York, 1960. [344]
Brief references to the major satires.

Yunck, John A. "The Skeptical Faith of Jonathan Swift," *Per-* [345]
sonalist, XLII (1961), 533–554.
Swift's beliefs were basically close to those of Pascal and
Dryden; all three profoundly questioned man's ability to use
his reason and later assented to religion. Swift's beliefs have
been both supplemented and obscured by his habitual fierce
irony, misanthropy, contempt, exaggeration; by his hatred of
speculative, systematic or subtle argument; and by his avoid-
ance of doctrinal topics. See Pons (285).

See (61), (64), (65), (66), (67), (69), (76), (84), (86), (90),
(101), (104), (111), (114), (128), (129), (133), (134), (145),
(352), (358), (359), (360), (362), (363), (368), (371), (373),
(374), (376), (390), (392), (394), (397), (403), (413), (417),
(420), (430), (434), (437), (442), (449), (488), (490), (502),
(509), (515), (519), (542), (563), (580), (581), (593), (596),
(597), (601), (614), (618), (620), (643), (645).

IV

Poetry

" 'A Beautiful Young Nymph Going to Bed'," *Johnsonian News* [346]
Letter, X (1950), No. 1, 7–8.
    An explication.

Bateson, F. W. "Swift's 'Description of the Morning'," in *Eng-* [347]
lish Poetry: A Critical Introduction. London and New York,
1950, pp. 175–178.
    A perceptive analysis of the poem and a brief discussion of
Swift's satire in terms of his audience. See Clark (349).

Bewley, Marius. "The Poetry of Swift," *Spectator*, August 29, [348]
1958, pp. 283–284.
    Review-article. See Horrell (54), Raymond (376).

Clark, William Ross. "Poems for Teaching: 'A Description of [349]
the Morning'," *Clearing House*, XXXV (February 1961),
381–382.
    A brief explication. See Bateson (347).

Colum, Padriac. "Return to the Poetry of Jonathan Swift," [350]
Pennsylvania Literary Review, Second Quarter (1955), 19–
26.
    Recommends Swift as a model "that would be compact and
orderly, that would be capable of dealing with the concrete
and somewhat acclimatised to metropolitan life."

Cox, Mary E. "Realism and Convention: A Study of the Poetry   [351]
of Prior, Swift, and Gay," Unpublished dissertation, Ohio
State University, 1960.
  See *DA*, XXI (1961), 2272–2273.

Davis, Herbert. "Alecto's Whip," *REL*, III (1962), 7–17.   [352]
  Swift is viewed as a "moralist aiming rather to heal than
  to hurt."

———. "A Modest Defence of 'The Lady's Dressing Room'," in   [353]
*Restoration and Eighteenth-Century Literature: Essays in
Honor of Alan Dugald McKillop* (Edited by Carroll Camden). Chicago, 1963, pp. 39–48.
  Discusses Swift's "obscene" poems and claims for Swift the
  prose tract entitled *A Modest Defense of a late Poem . . . called
  the Lady's Dressing Room.* See Woolley (49).

Dustin, John E. "The 1735 Dublin Edition of Swift's *Poems*,"   [354]
PBSA, LIV (1960), 57–60.
  Raises doubts about Faulkner's dating of the poems.

Ehrenpreis, Irvin. "Swift's First Poem," *MLR*, XLIX (1954),   [355]
210–211.
  "Ode to the King." See Jarrell (358).

Elwood, John R. "Swift's 'Corinna'," *N&Q*, CC, N.S. II (1955),   [356]
529–530.
  Believes that Mrs. E. Heywood is the model for Corinna.

Hone, Joseph M. "The Story of the Damer Gold," *Studies*,   [357]
XXXIX (1950), 419–426.
  Concerns Swift's "An Elegy on the much lamented death
  of Damer. . . ."

Jarrell, Mackie L. " 'Ode to the King': Some Contests, Dissen-   [358]
sions, and Exchanges among Jonathan Swift, John Dutton,
and Henry Jones," *TSLL*, VII (1965), 145–159.
  See Ehrenpreis (355).

Johnson, Maurice. *The Sin of Wit: Jonathan Swift as a Poet.* [359]
Syracuse, 1950.
Reviewed by O. W. Ferguson, *JEGP*, L (1951), 425–426;
H. Williams, *PQ*, XXX (1951), 294–295; B. Dobrée, *RES*,
III (1952), 89–90; C. Kulisheck, *MLQ*, XIII (1952), 105–106;
J. R. Sutherland, *MLN*, LXVIII (1953), 69–71. See Clifford
(191).

———. "Swift's Renunciation of the Muse," *N&Q*, CXCVII [360]
(1952), 235–236.
Discovers a precedent for Swift in Temple.

———. " 'Verses on the Death of Dr. Swift'," *N&Q*, CXCIX, [361]
N.S. I (1954), 473–474.
See Scouten (32) and Teerink (38) and (39). Also Slepian
(383) and Waingrow (386).

Johnston, Oswald. "Swift and the Common Reader," in *In De-* [362]
fense of Reading: A Reader's Approach to Literary Criticism
(Edited by R. A. Brower and Richard Poirier). New York,
1962, pp. 174–190.
Finds Swift refusing to fulfill any conventional expecta-
tions. His prose is notorious for its tricks and pitfalls: the
more one relies on the conventional attitude of reverence for
the classics and for the moral values of poetry, the more one
is likely to be ridiculed.

Kulisheck, Clarence L. "Swift's Poems about Women," *John-* [363]
sonian News Letter, X (1950), No. 3, 11–12.
Suggests that Book IV of Lucretius' *De Rerum Natura* is
good evidence that Swift is following a recognizable literary
convention in his scatological poems about women.

———. "Hudibrastic Echoes in Swift," *N&O*, CXCVI (1951), [364]
339.
See Kulisheck (365).

———. "Swift's Octosyllabics and the Hudibrastic Tradition," [365]
JEGP, LIII (1954), 361–368.

Influence of Butler on Swift parallels that of the blank verse of *Tamburlaine* on *Gorboduc*. See Kulisheck (364).

Mabbott, Thomas. " 'Bounce to Fop' by Swift and Pope," *N&Q*, [366] CC, N.S. II (1955), 433.
Concerns the line "Tho' some of J——'s hungry Breed." J—— refers to father of whelps of Pope's big dog who is supposed to be writing the poem.

Maxwell, Desmond E. S. "Poetic Inception," in *American Fic-* [367] *tion: The Intellectual Background*. New York, 1963, pp. 19–24.
Views Swift as an exile who can yet do the state some service through his art. His verse is for the most part a ruthless stripping of social and literary artifices. He envisages abstract vice primarily in abstract particulars, not in an intellectual void.

Miner, Earl R. "A Poem by Swift and W. B. Yeats' *Words upon* [368] *the Window-Pane*," *MLN*, LXXII (1957), 273–275.
Concerns "Written upon Windows at Inns, in England," a poem attributed to Swift.

O'Hehir, Brendan. "Meaning in Swift's 'Description of a City [369] Shower'," *ELH*, XXVII (1960), 194–207.
The poem's import seems to be within its own terms and to be primarily an oblique denunciation of the corruption of the city.

Ohlin, Peter. " 'Cadenus and Vanessa': Reason and Passion," [370] *SEL*, IV (1964), 485–496.
The poem is a delicately executed dialogue between reason and passion, utilizing the conflict between the principles as the controlling device. Swift is mocking the romantic cult of passionate love.

Paulson, Ronald. "Swift, Stella and Permanence," *ELH*, XXVII [371]
(1960), 298–314.
Poems are discussed to show Swift's "preoccupation with mutability."

Peake, Charles. "Swift's 'Satirical Elegy on a Late Famous Gen- [372]
eral'," *REL*, III (1962), 80–89.
The poem has emotional power, wit, a compact and logical structure, appropriate and unified imagery and tone, controlled variation of diction and movement—a wholeness in conception and execution not unworthy of a great writer like Swift.

Priestly, F. E. L. "Science and the Poet," *Dalhousie Review*, [373]
XXXVIII (1958), 141–153.
Refers to Swift, Green, Armstrong, Young, and Akenside.

Quinlan, Maurice J. "Swift and the Prosecuted Nottingham [374]
Speech," *HLB*, XI (1957), 296–302.
Concerns Swift's 54-line ballad on the subject.

Rawson, C. J. " 'The Vanity of Human Wishes,' Line 73: A [375]
Parallel from Swift," *N&Q*, CCX, N.S. XII (1965) 20–21.
See Ricks (378).

Raymond, John. "The Excremental Vision," *New Statesman*, [376]
January 4, 1958, pp. 735–736.
Review-article. See Horrell (54), Bewley (348).

Ricks, Christopher. "A Debt of Pope to Swift," *N&Q*, CCIV, [377]
N.S. VI (1959), 398–399.
Lines in Pope's "First Epistle of the Second Book of Horace" and "First Satire of the Second Book of Horace" suggested passages in Swift's "Directions for a Birth-day Song."

————. "Notes on Swift and Johnson," *RES*, XI (1960), 412–413. [378]
What is considered to be a mistranslation in his "Verses on

the Death of Dr. Swift" in the beginning maxim by La Roche-
foucauld is actually a reminiscence of a song by George
Granville; moveover, Johnson's line "They crowd about Preferment's Gate" is a borrowing from Swift. See Rawson
(375).

San Juan, E,. Jr. "The Anti-Poetry of Jonathan Swift," *PQ,*   [379]
XLIV (1965), 387–396.
"The anti-poetic element manifests itself in the intense
awareness of a unifying sensibility. . . . He exploited the
spiritual implications, values, and attitudes that facts pro-
voked, until finally consciousness became conscience."

Sherburn, George. "The Swift-Pope *Miscellanies* of 1732,"   [380]
HLB, VI (1952), 387–390.
A document of Swift throws light on the confusion sur-
rounding the publication of the final volume. See Sherburn
(381).

———. "The Swift-Pope *Miscellanies* of 1732: a Corrigendum,"   [381]
HLB, VII (1953), 248.
Concerned with the publication. See Sherburn (380).

Sinclair, Reid B. " 'What the World Calls Obscene': Swift's   [382]
'Ugly' Verse and the Satiric Tradition," Unpublished disser-
tation, Vanderbilt University, 1965.
See *DA,* XXVI (1966), 1028–1029.

Slepian, Barry. "The Ironic Intention of Swift's Verses on His   [383]
Own Death," *RES,* XIV (1963), 249–256.
See Waingrow (386). Also, see Scouten (32), Teerink
(38), Johnson (361).

Smith, T. Henry. "Swift's 'The Day of Judgment'," *Explicator,*   [384]
XXII (1963), Item 6.
A line by line analysis.

Tyne, James L. "The Misanthrope and the Muse: Swift's Lapi- [385]
dary Verse," Unpublished dissertation, Yale University, 1962.

Waingrow, Marshall. " 'Verses on the Death of Dr. Swift'," [386]
SEL, V (1965), 513–518.
See Slepian (383). Also, see Scouten (32), Teerink (38)
and (39), Johnson (361).

Waller, Charles T. "The Political Poetry of Jonathan Swift: A [387]
Critical Study," Unpublished dissertation, University of Pitts-
burgh, 1965.
See *DA*, XXVI (1966), 3966.

Wilson, Edmund. "Cousin Swift, You Will Never Be a Poet," [388]
in *Shores of Light: A Literary Chronicle of the Twenties and
Thirties*. New York, 1952, pp. 696–700.
Stresses the sensuous aspects of Swift's poetry and observes
that Swift created a new kind of lyric incorporating sneers
and curses.

See (9), (16), (19), (24), (25), (26), (28), (30), (32), (35),
(36), (38), (39), (53), (54), (55), (76), (107), (120), (122),
(133), (134), (163), (180), (204), (211), (232), (241), (252),
(289), (290), (294), (303), (340), (342).

V

Prose Writings

A. *The Battle of the Books*

Aden, John M. "Dryden and Swift," *N&Q*, CC, N.S. II (1955), [389]
239–240.
Two possible borrowings from Dryden in *The Battle of the Books* and *A Tale of a Tub*.

Green, David B. "Keats, Swift and Pliny the Elder," *N&Q*, [390]
CXCV (1950), 499–501.
Concerns the spider-bee metaphor. See Johnson (392).

Highet, Gilbert. "Battle of the Books," in *Classical Tradition:* [391]
Greek and Roman Influences on Western Literature. Oxford,
1949, pp. 261–288.
Discusses the academic battle between tradition and modernism, originality and authority. Concludes that the real fighting took place in France, but the work produced by English writers were more permanently interesting. Although Swift is discussed only briefly, the essay is important in placing *The Battle of the Books* in its proper historical perspective.

Johnson, James W. "That Neo-Classical Bee," *JHI*, XXII [392]
(1961), 262–266.
See Green (390).

Limouze, A. Sanford. "A Note on Virgil and *The Battle of the*   [393]
  Books," PQ, XXVII (1948), 85–89.
    Swift derived the framework of the Bentley-Wotton epi-
sode from Virgil. He wrote the mock epic similes in iambic
pentameter though presenting them as prose.

Pinkus, Philip. "Swift and the Ancients-Moderns Controversy,"   [394]
  UTQ, XXIX (1959), 46–58.
    Swift's main concern is not with the Ancients and Moderns.
"He is not the arch-conservative who can brook no charge,
condemning all modernity because it is new. He is the gentle-
man and man of taste, the humanist and man of religion, the
man of abundant sense who attacks whatever he considers to
be a breach of his essentially moral and religious standard. . . .
But essentially Swift's satire is a universal attack directed
against a universal target."

  See (58), (76), (180), (197), (200), (211), (264), (289),
(294), (303), (314), (326), (342), (343).

B. *A Tale of a Tub*

Andreasen, N. J. C. "Swift's Satire on the Occult in *A Tale of a*   [395]
  Tub," TSLL, V (1963), 410–421.
    Henry More's attack on the occultism of Thomas Vaughan
is paralleled in Swift's attitude toward his "occultist" persona.
See Pinkus (415).

Baker, Donald C. "Metaphors in Swift's *A Tale of a Tub* and   [396]
  Middleton's *The Family of Love*," N&Q, CCIII, N.S. V
  (1958), 107–108.
    Concerns principally the clothes metaphor used by Swift in
Sections II and VIII and by Middleton in Act IV, i.

Chiasson, Elias J. "Swift's Clothes Philosophy in the *Tale* and   [397]
  Hooker's Concept of Law," SP, LIX (1962), 64–82.
    Considers Hooker a decided influence.

Clark, John R. "*Fiat Nox*: The Nature of Satiric Creation;   [398]
  Study of Art and Tradition in Swift's *Tale of a Tub*," Un-

published dissertation, University of Michigan, 1965. See *DA*, XXVI (1966), 6710.

Duncan-Jones, E. E. "Joseph's Party-Coloured Coat and *A Tale* [399] *of a Tub*," *N&Q*, CCVI, N.S. VIII (1961), 251.
 Suggests that one of Thomas Fuller's sermons may be Swift's source for the coats covered with lace.

Elliott, Robert C. "Swift's *Tale of a Tub*: An Essay in Problems [400] of Structure," *PMLA*, LXVI (1951), 441–455.
 See review by E. W. Rosenheim, Jr., *PQ*, XXXI (1952), 302–303.

French, David P. "The Title of *A Tale of a Tub*," *N&Q*, [401] CXCVI (1951), 473–474.
 Meanings: (1) "an idle fiction;" (2) "a decoy designed to create a diversion;" (3) "the nonsensical ravings of a madman."

————. "Swift, Temple, and 'A Digression on Madness'," *TSLL*, [402] V (1963), 42–57.
 The digression reflects Swift's conflict between the opposing forces of a philosophical skepticism derived from Temple and traditional rationalism.

Harth, Phillip. *Swift and Anglican Rationalism: The Religious* [403] *Background of "A Tale of a Tub."* Chicago and London, 1961.
 Reviews: H. Davis, *RES*, XIII (1962), 413–414; R. Paulson, *JEGP*, LXI (1962), 406–408; E. Pons, *EA*, XV (1962), 187–188; R. Quintana, *MP*, LX (1962), 141–143; H. Trowbridge, *PQ*, XLI (1962), 630–631; C. H. Cable, *Criticism*, V (1963), 87–88; D. P. French, *BA*, XXXVII (1963), 160–163.

Horne, Colin J., and Hugh Powell. "A German Analogue for *A* [404] *Tale of a Tub*," *MLR*, LV (1960), 488–496.
 Martin Rinckhart's *Der Eislebische Christliche Ritter*, 1613.

Hughes, R. E. "The Five Fools in *A Tale of a Tub*," *Literature* [405] *and Psychology*, XI (1961), 20–22.
 Finds Swift analyzing five degrees of madness.

Kelling, H. D. "Reason and Madness in *A Tale of a Tub*," [406]
PMLA, LXIX (1954), 198–222.
Suggests that the *Tale* has a central subject not too unlike
the subject of Joyce's *Portrait*. It is still relevant because the
characteristics of sophistic rhetoric have not changed and the
principles of rational rhetoric are still valid. See Kenner (407).

Kenner, Hugh. *Flaubert, Joyce, and Beckett, the Stoic Come-* [407]
dians. Boston, 1962, pp. 37–42.
Treats *A Tale of a Tub* as a parody of the book as a book,
"the register of Gutenburg technology, discerned by a man
who regarded each of the bookmaker's devices as a monstrous
affront to the personal intercourse which letters . . . had served
to promote." See Kelling (406).

Maxwell, J. C. "*A Tale of a Tub*: A Correction," *N&Q*, CXCV [408]
(1950), 249.
Explains an allusion in Section II.

———. "The Text of *A Tale of a Tub*," *English Studies*, XXXVI [409]
(1955), 64–66.
Intends to show that Herbert Davis has failed to restore
quite a number of evidently correct readings in the fifth edition of 1710.

Miller, Henry K. "The Paradoxical Encomium with Special [410]
Reference to Its Vogue in England, 1600–1800," *MP*, LIII
(1956), 145–178.
A history of the rhetorical jest.

Moore, John R. "A Possible Model for the Organization of [411]
A Tale of a Tub," *N&Q*, CXCIX, N.S. I (1954), 288–290.
John Ray's *Miscellaneous Discourses Concerning the Disso-
lution of the World*, 1692.

Olson, R. C. "Swift's Use of the *Philosophical Transactions* in [412]
Section V of *A Tale of a Tub*," *SP*, XLIX (1952), 459–467.
See a review by E. Rosenheim, Jr., *PQ*, XXXII (1953), 296.

Paulson, Ronald. *Theme and Structure in Swift's "Tale of a* [413]
Tub." New Haven, 1960.
　　Reviews: F. Brady, *YR*, XLIX (1960), 598–602; H. Davis,
RES, XII (1961), 300–302; S. A. Golden, *Criticism*, III (1961),
254–258; P. Harth, *MP*, LVIII (1961), 282–285; S. Hawkins,
MLN, LXXVI (1961), 462–464; M. Starkman, *MLQ*, XXII
(1961), 90–91; E. Rosenheim, Jr., *PQ*, XL (1961), 430–433;
K. Williams, *JEGP*, LX (1961), 587–589.

Pinkus, Philip. "The Nature of the Satire in *A Tale of a Tub*," [414]
Unpublished dissertation, University of Michigan, 1956.
　　See *DA*, XVII (1957), 145–146.

———. "*A Tale of a Tub* and the Rosy Cross," *JEGP*, LIX [415]
(1960), 669–679.
　　Rosicrucianism as one of the major unifying devices in
A Tale. See Andreasen (395).

———. "The Upside-down World of *A Tale of a Tub*," *Eng-* [416]
lish Studies, XLIV (1963), 161–175.
　　Discusses what kind of world the Tubbian world is and
how it comes about.

Quintana, Ricardo. "Emile Pons and the Modern Study of [417]
Swift's *Tale of a Tub*," *EA*, XVIII (1965), 5–17.
　　Discusses the various critical approaches to the work since
Pons' study.

Roscelli, William J. "*A Tale of a Tub* and the 'Cavils of the [418]
Sour'," *JEGP*, LXIV (1965), 41–56.
　　Finds much to justify the protests against Swift's apparent
acceptance of a rationalistic definition of faith which would
subject creed to the verification of reason.

Smith, Curtis C. "Metaphor Structure in Swift's *A Tale of a* [419]
Tub," *Thoth*, V (1964), 22–41.
　　Swift achieves satirical inversion through the use of an
"inner versus outer metaphor structure."

Starkman, Miriam. *Swift's Satire on Learning in "A Tale of a* [420]
Tub." Princeton, 1950.
Reviews: *TLS*, July 27, 1951, p. 464; E. Rosenheim, Jr.,
PQ, XXX (1951), 296–299; H. Williams, *RES*, V (1954),
86–87. See Clifford (191).

———. "Quakers, Phrenologists, and Jonathan Swift," *JHI*, XX [421]
(1959), 403–412.
A pamphlet published in Philadelphia (1826) entitled *Tale
of a Tub: Part Second* by "Democritus Americanus."

Stedmond, J. M. "Another Possible Analogue for Swift's *Tale* [422]
of a Tub," *MLN*, LXXII (1957), 13–18.
John Dunstan's *Voyage Round the World*, 1691.

Stephens, Lamarr. " 'A Digression in Praise of Digressions' As [423]
a Classical Oration: Rhetorical Satire in Section VII of Swift's
A Tale of a Tub," *TSE*, XIII (1963), 41–49.

Tague, Wilma L. "Stephen Gosson and 'Homer's Iliades in a [424]
Nutte Shell'," *N&Q*, CCV, N.S. VII (1960), 372–373.
On a phrase in Section VII of *A Tale*.

Teerink, Herman. "A Source-book for *A Tale of a Tub* from [425]
Swift's Own Library," *Irish Book Lover*, October 1949, pp.
59–62.
Mezeray's *Abrégé chronologique de l'histoire de France* as
a source for Chapter 9.

See (58), (59), (76), (180), (191), (200), (204), (215),
(223), (252), (289), (290), (294), (303), (311), (314), (326),
(340), (342), (343), (389).

C. The Mechanical Operation of the Spirit

Calderwood, James L. "Structural Parody in Swift's *Fragment*," [426]
MLQ, XXIII (1962), 243–253.

Swift's *Fragment* concludes as it began, in apparent confusion; the form is established by purely mechanical conformity to fashions of the moment.

Clifford, James L. "Swift's 'Mechanical Operation of the   [427]
Spirit'," in *Pope and His Contemporaries: Essays Presented
to George Sherburn* (Edited by James L. Clifford and Louis
A. Landa). Oxford, 1949, pp. 135–146.
Swift wanted to 'vex' mankind to show that the religious
imagination out of control is only a corruption of the senses.
He deliberately chose to end his attack with the most revolt-
ing bits of imagery. The operation of the spirit is wholly
physical. The *Discourse* was meant to be the true ending of
the whole complex system of *A Tale of a Tub*.

See (58), (180), (215), (252), (289), (303), (342).

D. Political Writings

Allen, Robert J. "Swift's *Contests and Dissensions* in Boston,"   [428]
New England Quarterly, XXIX (1956), 73–82.
Suggests reasons why Swift's pamphlet was reprinted in
Boston in 1728.

Cook, Richard I. "Dryden's 'Absalom and Achitophel' and   [429]
Swift's Political Tracts, 1710–1714," *HLQ*, XXIV (1961),
345–348.
Finds analogies.

———. "Swift as a Tory Rhetorician," *TSLL*, IV (1962), 72–86.   [430]
It is in terms of their persuasive goals that the tracts and the
role they play in Swift's career can be best understood.

———. "The 'Several Ways . . . of Abusing One Another': Jon-   [431]
athan Swift's Political Journalism," *Speech Monographs*,
XXIX (1962), 260–273.
Swift's pieces for the Tories used four techniques:
(1) nicknames and blanks for letters in real names to avoid

libel; (2) "putting cases," including laws the opposition might favor, anecdotes, analogies and key images of servants, family, sickness, usurers, etc.; (3) "insinuations"—pose of utter frankness while attributing hidden motives to opposition; (4) positive celebration of Tory acts.

———. "The Uses of *Saeva Indignatio*: Swift's Political Tracts [432] (1710–1714) and His Sense of Audience," *SEL*, II (1962), 287–307.

Swift's experience as a Tory propagandist and the Tory debacle of 1714 led him to write in the public spirit; after 1714 he was devoted to satirizing the Whigs and the evil forces they represented in his mind.

———. "The Audience of Swift's Tory Tracts, 1710–14," *MLQ*, [433] XXIV (1963), 31–41.

Studies the nature of Swift's audience from his references to them and from the tone and nature of his arguments. Swift's conscious efforts to cater to a rural readership mark a significant stage in the growth of his concept of audience.

Davis, Herbert. "Some Free Thoughts of a Tory Dean," *Vir-* [434] *ginia Quarterly Review*, XXVIII (1952), 258–272.

Swift remained a loyal Churchman and moderate Tory throughout his life. He was a moralist and had a humorous, satirical bent with little enthusiasm or sentiment either in religion or in politics.

Drozdowski, Eugene C. "Jonathan Swift, Political Propagandist, [435] 1710–1713," *Appalachian State Teachers College Faculty Publications*, 1962, pp. 3–34.

Swift as a Tory propagandist: wrote to justify the change in the government and to prepare the public for peace; defended the ministry when its negotiations with Louis XIV were revealed; attempted to bring factions together; and tried to obtain preferment.

Ehrenpreis, Irvin. "Swift's 'Enquiry'," *N&Q*, CXCIV (1949),   [436]
360.
   Annotation of a passage concerning Baron Hunsdon and
Mrs. Mary Foyston.

Jones, Myrddin. *"Further Thoughts on Religion*: Swift's Re-   [437]
lation to Filmer and Locke," *RES*, IX (1958), 284–286.
   Swift accepted Locke's position in *Two Treatises on Government* (1690). See Colie (515).

McAleer, John J. "Swift's Letcombe Admonition to Boling-   [438]
broke," *CLA Journal*, IV (1961), 188–195.
   Concerns *Some Free Thoughts Upon the Present State of
Affairs.*

Steensma, Robert C. "Swift on Standing Armies: A Possible   [439]
Source," *N&Q*, CCVIII, N.S. X (1963), 215–216.
   Cites Sir William Temple.

See (12), (37), (51), (58), (76), (180), (196), (200), (204),
(215), (286), (289), (294), (303), (342).

E. Historical Writings

Ehrenpreis, Irvin. "Swift's History of England," *JEGP*, LI   [440]
(1952), 177–185.
   A study of sources.

Mayhew, George P. "Swift's Notes for His *The History of the*   [441]
Last Four Years, Book IV," *HLQ*, XXIV (1961), 311–322.
   Huntington MS. No. 14380 is an unpublished series of six
notes for the *History*, which suggest that the *History* is indeed by Swift and show how exactly and painstakingly he
worked as a Tory historian to gather data.

Moore, John R. "Swift as Historian," *SP*, XLIX (1952), 583–   [442]
604.
   Swift's overemphasis on personal hearsay appears through-

out his historical writings; the brillant pamphleteer was never successfully submerged in the historian.

Sherman, Margaret E. *A Study of Swift's "History of the Last* [443] *Four Years of the Queen": As a History and As a Tory Document.* New York, 1955.

See (58), (196), (247), (289), (294).

F. *The Drapier's Letters* and Irish Tracts

Ferguson, Oliver W. *Jonathan Swift and Ireland.* Urbana, 1962. [444]
Reviews: H. L. Calkin, *American Historical Review*, LXVIII (1962), 508; J. C. Beckett, *Irish Historical Studies*, XIII (1963), 271–273; F. Brady, *YR*, LII (1963), 267–270; W. B. Fleischman, *BA*, XXXVII (1963), 74; V. Mercier, *HR*, XVI (1963), 290–296; C. J. Rawson, *N&Q*, CCVIII, N.S. X (1963), 478–479; J. G. Simms, *History*, XLVIII (1963), 79–80; D. T. Torchiana, *PQ*, XLII (1963), 377–379; A. J. Farmer, *Erasmus*, XV (1964), 671–674; L. Landa, *ELN*, I (1964), 226–227; K. Williams, *RES*, XV (1964), 205–206. See Johnston (110), Ferguson (450).

Gilbert, Jack G. "The Drapier's Initials," *N&Q*, CCVIII, N.S. [445]
X (1963), 217–218.
MB = Marcus Brutus.

Woodring, Carl R. "The Aims, Audience, and Structure of the [446]
Drapier's Fourth Letter," *MLQ*, XVII (1956), 50–59.
Intends "to demonstrate the effect of Swift's diverse aims and multifarious audience on the structure" while incidentally examining who were "the Whole People of Ireland?"

See (2), (58), (180), (200), (204), (215), (289), (294), (303), (342).

G. *A Modest Proposal*

Baker, Donald C. "Tertullian and Swift's 'A Modest Proposal'," [447]
Classical Journal, LII (1957), 219–220.
See Johnson (452).

Beaumont, Charles A. "Swift's Classical Rhetoric in 'A Modest   [448]
Proposal'," *Georgia Review*, XIV (1960), 307–317.
   The work exemplifies Swift's use of classical rhetoric in its
structure and development. The structure is that of a five-
part oration, and the main devices are ethical proof, diminu-
tion, and refining.

Cook, Richard I. "Defoe and Swift: Contrasts in Satire," *Dal-*   [449]
housie Review, XLIII (1963), 28–39.
   Compares Defoe's "Shortest Way with Dissenters" and
Swift's "Modest Proposal."

❧ Ferguson, Oliver W. "Swift's *Saeva Indignatio* and 'A Modest   [450]
Proposal'," *PQ*, XXXVIII (1959), 473–479.
   Ten years of warning and exhortation gave way to frustra-
tion and despair and here, stripped of all irony and grounded
in the authority of Scripture, is the moralist's judgment on the
people of Ireland. See Ferguson (444).

Greenberg, Robert A. "'A Modest Proposal' and the Bible,"   [451]
MLR, LV (1960), 568–569.
   Swift draws upon the Old Testament admonition that un-
less the Hebrews mend their ways they will be reduced
(amongst other extremities) to the eating of their children.
Cites the Biblical sources.

Johnson, James W. "Tertullian and 'A Modest Proposal',"   [452]
MLN, LXXIII (1958), 561–563.
   Tertullian's *Apologia* is the "most obvious and direct influence . . . stylistically as well as thematically. . . ." See Baker
(447).

Johnson, Maurice. "The Structural Impact of 'A Modest Pro-   [453]
posal'," *BuR*, VII (1958), 234–240.
   The work's unifying intensity is achieved through Swift's
use of a verbal contrivance, working throughout the structure: "the perpetual slight alteration of language." The ten-

sion in the work derives from the cumulative ironic effect of
Swift's phraseology.

Long, Littleton. "Swift's Arithmetic," *N&Q*, CCIII, N.S. V   [454]
(1958), 219.
    Lapses in "A Modest Proposal" and *Gulliver*.

See (58), (169), (180), (200), (212), (215), (252), (289),
(290), (294), (303), (314), (342).

H. *Polite Conversation*

Barker, Elizabeth: "Giovanni Battista Gelli's *Circe* and Jona-   [455]
than Swift," *Cesare Barbieri Courier* (Trinity College, Hart-
ford), II (1959), 3–15.
    See Jarrell (457).

Jarrell, Mackie L. "The Proverbs in Swift's *Polite Conversa-*   [456]
tion," *HLQ*, XX (1956), 15–38.
    Finds in Swift an amused contempt for empiricism and for
the cockle-shell collectors of the Royal Society.

———. "Joyce's Use of Swift's *Polite Conversation* in the 'Circe'   [457]
Episode of *Ulysses*," *PMLA*, LXXII (1957), 545–554.
    See Barker (455).

Mayhew, George. "Some Dramatizations of Swift's *Polite Con-*   [458]
versation (1738)," *PQ*, XLIV (1965), 51–72.
    Describes Swift's interest in stage drama and his possible
thought of adapting this work for stage presentation; examines various editions and dramatizations.

Osselton, N. E. "Butter for Fish," *English Studies*, XXXVIII   [459]
(1957), 266–267.
    Swift may mean "tit for tat."

See (22), (29), (56), (57), (58), (201), (204).

I. Correspondence and *Journal to Stella*

Donoghue, Denis. "A Note on Swift," *New Statesman*, November 1, 1963, pp. 877–878.   [460]
  Review-article; see Williams (50) and Hough (463).

Ehrenpreis, Irvin. "Swift's 'Little Language' in the *Journal to Stella*," *SP*, XLV (1948), 80–88.   [461]
  Discusses Swift's phonetic method.

———. "Lady Betty Butler to Swift," *TLS*, December 15, 1950, p. 801.   [462]
  Prints the only extant letter.

Hough, Graham. "Letters from Limbo," *The Spectator*, December 6, 1963, pp. 755–756.   [463]
  Review-article. See Williams (50) and Donoghue (460).

Milic, Louis T. " 'Vive la Bagatelle!'," *N&Q*, CC, N.S. II (1955), 363–364.   [464]
  Notes the source; Swift uses the expression "Vive la Bagatelle!" only in his letters.

Pritchett, Victor S. "Swift to Stella," in *Books in General*. New York, 1953, pp. 81–87.   [465]
  Review-article. See Williams (52) and Wilson (468). Finds the *Journal* intimate and revealing yet unbetraying.

Scouten, A. H. "Swift at the Moving Pictures," *N&Q*, CLXXXVIII (1945), 38–39.   [466]
  Annotation of a passage in the *Journal to Stella*.

Wills, Geoffrey. "Ceramic Causerie," *Apollo*, LXX (December 1959), 186.   [467]
  References to pottery and porcelain in the *Journal to Stella*.

Wilson, Edmund. "The Most Unhappy Man on Earth," in [468]
Classics and Commercials: A Literary Chronicle of the Forties.
New York, 1950, pp. 453–459.
   A review-article. See Williams (52) and Pritchett (465).

See (47), (50), (52), (106), (180), (189), (204), (289),
(317).

J. Miscellaneous Prose Writings

Bernard, F. V. "Swift's Maxim on Populousness: A Possible [469]
Source," *N&Q*, CCX, N.S. XII (1965), 18.
   Sir William Temple in "Of Popular Discontents" and in
"An Essay Upon the Advancement of Trade in Ireland."

Bond, Richmond P. "Isaac Bickerstaff, Esq.," in *Restoration* [470]
*and Eighteenth-Century Literature: Essays in Honor of Alan
Dugald McKillop* (Edited by Carroll Camden). Chicago,
1963, pp. 103–124.
   Swift's *persona* and Steele's.

———. "John Partridge and the Company of Stationers," *SB*, [471]
XVI (1963), 61–80.
   Bickerstaff Papers. See Mayhew (479).

Davis, Kathryn. "A Note on the *Spectator* 459," *MLN*, LX [472]
(1945), 274.
   On Addison quoting from Swift's *Thoughts on Various
Subjects.*

Ehrenpreis, Irvin. "The Date of Swift's 'Sentiments'," *RES*, [473]
III (1952), 272–274.
   Argues for 1704.

———. "The Literary Side of a Satirist's Work," *Minnesota* [474]
Review, II (1962), 179–197.
   Treats *An Argument against Abolishing Christianity.*

Erickson, Robert A. "Situations of Identity in the *Memoirs of*   [475]
Martinus Scriblerus," *MLQ*, XXVI (1965), 388–400.
    Swift, Arbuthnot, and Pope shared the view of man as a di-
vided animal. But the ultimate definition in the *Memoirs* is not
man the divided animal, but man the absurd animal.

Huxley, Herbert H. "*Sanguis equinus* (Virgil Georg. 3. 463)   [476]
and Dean Swift," *Classical Philology*, LIV (1959), 122.
    A note to a passage in the *Answer to the "Craftsman."*

Kerby-Miller, Charles (Editor). *Memoirs of the Extraordinary*   [477]
Life, Works, and Discoveries of Martinus Scriblerus. London,
1950.
    Reviews. D. Cornu, *MLQ*, XI (1950), 502–504; H. Davis,
PQ, XXX (1951), 254–256; W. H. Irving, *SAQ*, L (1951),
152–153.

McKillop, Alan Dugald. "The Geographical Chapter in *Scrib-*   [478]
lerus," *MLN*, LXVIII (1953), 480–481.
    Notes that Bernhardus Varenius' *Geographia Generalis*
is the principal source.

Mayhew, George P. "The Early Life of John Partridge," *SEL*,   [479]
I (1961), 31–42.
    Bickerstaff Papers. See Bond (471).

———. "Jonathan Swift's Hoax of 1722 Upon Ebenezor Elliston,"   [480]
BJRL, XLIV (1962), 360–380.
    Similar to Swift's hoax on Partridge (*Bickerstaff Papers*).

———. "Swift's Bickerstaff Hoax as an April Fools' Joke," *MP*,   [481]
LXI (1964), 270–280.
    Demonstrates that Swift's four-part joke on Partridge was
an April Fools' joke.

Quinlan, Maurice J. "Swift's *Project for the Advancement of* [482]
Religion and the Reformation of Manners," *PMLA*, LXXI
(1956), 201–212.
Considers the influence that led Swift to write it, the em-
phasis in the essay, and his position at the time he composed it.

Rawson, C. J. "Swift's Certificate to Parnell's *Posthumous* [483]
Works," *MLR*, LVII (1962), 179–182.
Concludes that the volume and the preface by Swift are
genuine.

———. "A Phrase of John Gay in Swift's *Modest Defence of The* [484]
Lady's Dressing-Room?" *RES*, XVI (1965), 406–407.
A letter of Gay, dated March 1716, includes words reap-
pearing in Swift's pamphlet.

Stathis, James J. "Swift and the Rhetoric of Reason: A Study of [485]
the Sermons," Unpublished dissertation, University of Wisconsin, 1964.
See *DA*, XXV (1964), 2988–2989.

Steeves, Edna Leake (Editor). *The Art of Sinking in Poetry:* [486]
Martinus Scriblerus' "Peri Bathos." A Critical Edition with
Bibliographical Notes on the Last Volume of the Swift–
Pope *Miscellanies* by R. H. Griffith and E. L. Steeves. New
York and London, 1952.
Reviewed by B. Boyce, *SAQ*, LI (1952), 619; C. Kerby-
Miller, *PQ*, XXXII (1953), 286–288.

See (3), (4), (5), (8), (11), (14), (15), (20), (21), (34),
(43), (49), (58), (128), (129), (136), (141), (169), (180),
(204), (215), (289), (290), (294), (303), (342).

VI

Gulliver's Travels

Adams, Percy G. *Travelers and Travel Liars, 1660–1800.* Berke- [487]
ley, 1962.
   "The story of Gulliver is itself the great English example
of the imaginary or extraordinary voyage."

Adams, Robert M. "Swift and Kafka," in *Strains of Discord:* [488]
Studies in Literary Openness. Ithaca, N.Y., 1958, pp. 146–179.
   See Neumeyer (593).

Baker, Sheridan. "Swift, 'Lilliputian,' and Catullus," *N&Q,* CCI, [489]
N.S. III (1956), 477–479.
   Catullus may have provided Swift with a model for the
word, Lilliputian. Related Studies: Bracher (497), Brandt
(498), Clark (513), Cornelius (517), Kelling (561), Moore
(588), Pons (600), Richer (607), Seeber (617), Seronsy
(619).

Ball, Albert. "Swift and the Animal Myth," *Transactions of the* [490]
Wisconsin Academy of Sciences, Arts, and Letters, XLVIII
(1959), 239–248.
   An attempt to regard Swift's art in the light of the happy
beast tradition, particularly as it is developed in French
thought.

Banks, Loy O. "Moral Perspective in *Gulliver's Travels* and [491]
    Candide: Broadsword and Rapier?" *Forum* (Houston), IV
    (1965), 4–8.
    Concerns "several differences in moral perspective, per-
spective that is as different as the Saxon and the Gallic tem-
perament."

Barroll, J. Leeds. "Gulliver in Luggnagg: A Possible Source," [492]
    PQ, XXXVI (1957), 504–508.
    E. Kaempfer's *The History of Japan* (1727).

——. "Gulliver and the Struldbruggs," *PMLA*, LXXIII (1958), [493]
    43–50.
    Considers three aspects of the Struldbrugg episode: (1) old
age and the fear of death as conventional subjects for moral
reflection and satire; (2) a desire for immortality in the light
of the homiletic tradition; (3) the significance of Gulliver's
conversations with his host.

Benjamin, Edwin B. "The King of Brobdingnag and *Secrets of* [494]
    State," *JHI*, XVIII (1957), 572–579.
    Echoes of Tacitus and Machiavelli.

Block, Edward A. "Lemuel Gulliver: Middle-class English- [495]
    man," *MLN*, LXVIII (1953), 474–477.
    The reader's awareness of Gulliver's universality and time-
lessness stems out of his prior recognition that Gulliver represents the average Englishman.

Bloom, Allan. "An Outline of *Gulliver's Travels*" in *Ancients* [496]
    and Moderns: Essays on the Tradition of Political Philosophy
    in Honor of Leo Strauss (Edited by Joseph Cropsey). New
    York, 1964, pp. 238–258.

Bracher, Frederick. "The Name 'Lemuel Gulliver'," *HLQ*, XII [497]
    (1949), 409–413.
    The name is a synthetic compound with no meaning ex-

cept the hint in the first syllable. Related Studies: Baker (489), Brandt (498), Clark (513), Cornelius (517), Kelling (561), Moore (588), Pons (600), Richer (607), Seeber (617), Seronsy (619).

Brandt, E. H. "Some Proper Names in *Gulliver's Travels*,"   [498]
N&Q, CCIII, N.S. V (1958), 44.
    See particularly Seronsy (619). Related Studies: Baker (489), Bracher (497), Clark (513), Cornelius (517), Kelling (561), Moore (588), Pons (600), Richer (607), Seeber (617).

Brinton, Henry C. "Swift's Forecast of Mars' Satellites," *Sky*   [499]
and Telescope, XV (September 1956), 494.

Brown, William J. "Gulliver's Passage on the Dutch *Amboyna*,"   [500]
ELN, I (1964), 262–264.
    On one of Swift's sharpest sallies against the Dutch—a reference to a tradition of their brutality toward the English, a tradition so long and firmly established that the single word "Amboyna" was sufficient to revive it. See Clark (188), Leyburn (256).

Bruckmann, Patricia. "Gulliver, *Cum Grano Salis*," *Satire*   [501]
Newsletter, I (1963), 5–11.
    Gulliver and food, particularly salt.

Burian, Orhan. "Da Vinci and Swift," *N&Q*, CXCVII (1952),   [502]
451–452.
    On a letter of da Vinci to Benedetto d' Pentarli which bears on Gulliver's first experience in Lilliput.

Burns, Wayne. "Our Heritage from a Great Book," *School and*   [503]
Society, LXIV (October 1946), 235–237.
    A satiric examination of the "prophetic" nature of Part II, Chapter 7 of *Gulliver's Travels* as a commentary on the "common heritage" theory of the "great books" advocates.

Byers, John R., Jr. "Another Source for *Gulliver's Travels*," [504]
JEGP, LVII (1958), 14–20.
H. Hamel's "An Account of the Shipwreck of a Dutch
Vessel."

Calkins, Ernest E. "How Small is Lilliput?" *Atlantic Monthly*, [505]
July 1952, pp. 77–78.
Examines Swift's references to size to see whether or not he
is good at scale models.

Carnochan, W. B. "*Gulliver's Travels*: An Essay on the Human [506]
Understanding?" *MLQ*, XXV (1954), 5–21.
Argues that the *Travels* are as much concerned with human
understanding as they are with man in an abstract definition.

———. "Some Roles of Lemuel Gulliver," *TSLL*, V (1954), [507]
520–529.
Gulliver's important and interlocking roles as surgeon and
physician, court fool, "archetypal victim," and myopic hero
help to anticipate his change from innocence to misanthropy.
In his progression toward a realization of the possibilities of
these roles, he achieves an "ironic version of the myth in
which the hero at last comes face-to-face with the monster."

———. "The Complexity of Swift: Gulliver's Fourth Voyage," [508]
SP, LX (1963), 23–44.
Views Swift as a frustrated idealist and the Houyhnhnms
as his intended ideal.

Case, Arthur E. *Four Essays on "Gulliver's Travels."* Princeton, [509]
N.J., 1945.
Reviews: D. Cornu, *MLQ*, VII (1946), 505–506; H. Davis,
PQ, XXV (1946), 164–167; W. H. Irving, *SAQ*, XLV (1946),
393–394; R. F. Jones, *MLN*, LXII (1947), 206–208; R. Quin-
tana, *JEGP*, XLVI (1947), 322–324; G. Sherburn, *YR*, XXXV
(1946), 760–761; H. Williams, *RES*, XXIII (1947), 367–369.
See Fink (530).

Casey, B. H. "The Misanthrope in English Literature of the   [510]
Eighteenth Century," Unpublished dissertation, University
of Texas, 1962.
See *DA*, XXIII (1962), 1683–1684.

Catlin, Fulton. "Swift's Moral Realism in *Gulliver's Travels*,"   [511]
Abstracts of Dissertations, University of Wisconsin, XIII
(1953), 377–378.

Churchill, R. C. *English Literature of the Eighteenth Century,*   [512]
With a Preface on the Relations Between Literary History
and Literary Criticism. London, 1953, pp. 53–59.
Gulliver is briefly discussed in a general and rather superficial fashion.

Clark, Paul O. "A Gulliver Dictionary," *SP*, L (1953), 592–624.   [513]
See a review by M. Price, *PQ*, XXXIII (1954), 301–302.
Related Studies: Baker (489), Bracher (497), Brandt (498),
Cornelius (517), Kelling (561), Moore (588), Pons (600),
Richer (607), Seeber (617), Seronsy (619).

———. "Lapponia, Lapland and Laputa," *MLQ*, XIX (1958),   [514]
343–351.
On the possible influence of Defoe's *Consolidator.*

Colie, Rosalie L. "Gulliver, the Locke-Stillingfleet Contro-   [515]
versy, and the Nature of Man," *History of Ideas News Letter*,
II (1956), 58–62.
On Locke's influence. See Jones (437).

Corder, Jim. "Gulliver in England," *CE*, XXIII (1961), 98–103.   [516]
The actual setting is England—only Gulliver's point of view
varies. The reader is asked to look at familiar beings from an
unfamiliar point of view.

Cornelius, Paul E. "Language in Seventeenth- and Early Eigh-   [517]
teenth-Century Imaginary Voyages," Unpublished dissertation, Columbia University, 1962.

See *DA*, XXIII (1963), 3351. Related Studies: Baker (489), Bracher (497), Brandt (498), Clark (513), Kelling (561), Moore (588), Pons (600), Richer (607), Seeber (617), Seronsy (619).

Crane, R. S. "The Rationale of the Fourth Voyage," in *Jonathan* [518] *Swift: Gulliver's Travels* (Edited by R. A. Greenberg). New York, 1961, pp. 300–307.
Gulliver should not be read in a Christian context; it is not an allegory but a "fantastic fable."

——. "The Houyhnhnms, the Yahoos, and the History of [519] Ideas," in *Reason and the Imagination: Studies in the History of Ideas, 1600–1800* (Edited by J. A. Mazzeo). New York and London, 1962, pp. 231–253.
Swift aims his satire, in part, at the logician's definition of man as *animal rationale*; Book IV, then, is "in considerable part at least, an anti-Porphyrian satire."

Danchin, Pierre. "Le Lecteur Anglais d'Aujourd'hui Peut-il [520] Connaître *Gulliver's Travels?*" *EA*, XI (1958), 97–111.
Critical examination of eight modern editions.

——. "The Text of *Gulliver's Travels*," *TSLL*, II (1960), 233– [521] 250.
See Williams (650) and (651); also Todd (641).

Dircks, Richard J. "Gulliver's Tragic Rationalism," *Criticism*, [522] II (1960), 134–149.
The impact on him of the world of perfect reason (Book IV) drives Gulliver insane.

Dobrin, Milton B. "Lilliput Revisited: Reynolds, Fronde, Di- [523] mensional Analysis, and Dean Swift," *Technology Review*, XLVII (1945), 299–300 and 320–326.
Discusses all the dimensional relationships that Swift uses.

Downs, Robert Bingham. "The Damned Human Race," in [524]
Molders of the Modern Mind; 111 Books That Shaped Western Civilization. New York, 1961, pp. 115–119.

Ehrenpreis, Irvin. "The Origin of *Gulliver's Travels*," *PMLA*, [525]
LXXII (1957), 880–899.
   Argues from evidence in Swift's correspondence that the origins are not the Scriblerus papers but that during the years just before writing *Gulliver*, Swift was putting together unpublished essays on English politics (mainly from 1708–1715) and that he created *Gulliver* out of his own memories, experiences, and reflections from 1714–1725. The ruler of Lilliput descended from Bolingbroke and the king of Part II is modeled mainly on Temple; in Part IV Swift was aiming at deistic thought and Bolingbroke in particular; Swift's friend Thomas Sheridan was the model for the King of Laputa. Reviewed by R. Quintana, *PQ*, XXXVII (1958), 354–355; also Sherburn (623).

———. "The Meaning of Gulliver's Last Voyage," *REL*, III [526]
(1962), 18–38.
   Addressed to those who might not only regard the character of a Houyhnhnm as admirable but also treat it as an easy ideal for humanity.

Elliott, Robert C. "Gulliver as a Literary Artist," *ELH*, XIX [527]
(1952), 49–63.
   Gulliver turns out to be an accomplished literary artist, capable of self-insight, objectivity, and perhaps even irony.

———. "Gulliver's Travels," in *The Power of Satire: Magic,* [528]
Ritual, and Art. Princeton, N.J., 1960, pp. 184–222.

Eves, Howard. "The Astonishing Prediction in *Gulliver's Travels*," *The Mathematics Teacher*, LIV (December 1961), 625– [529]
626.

The astronomical achievements of the Laputians are re-
markably prophetic of the discoveries American astronomer
Asaph Hall made 150 years after *Gulliver's* publication.

Fink, Z. S. "Political Theory in *Gulliver's Travels*," ELH, XIV [530]
(1947), 151–161.
Discusses the development of the idea of the balanced state
and its place in Swift's political thought. See Case (509).

Foster, Milton P. (Editor). *A Casebook on Gulliver among the* [531]
Houyhnhnms. New York, 1961.
A collection of important previously published essays. Re-
viewed by A. E. Dyson, *MLR*, LVII (1962), 420–421.

Frédérix, Pierre. *Swift, le Véritable Gulliver*. Paris, 1964. [532]
See review by J. Béranger, *EA*, XVIII (1965), 187–189.

French, David P. "The Swift-Gulliver Litigation," *N&Q*, XI [533]
(1964), 52–53.
Documents of 1733–1748 in Westminster Abbey, in which
Lemuel Gulliver accused one Peter Swift, reflect the popu-
larity of Swift's book, not the source of his proper names.

Frietzsche, A. H. "The Impact of Applied Science Upon the [534]
Utopian Ideal," *Brigham Young University Studies*, III
(1961), 35–42.
Treats More, Bacon, and *Gulliver*, Book III.

Frye, Roland M. "Swift's Yahoos and the Christian Symbols for [535]
Sin," *JHI*, XV (1954), 201–217.
The description of the Yahoos includes many of the physi-
cal traits associated with sin and depravity by religious writers
of the sixteenth and seventeenth centuries. See Brown (178),
Murray (591).

Fussell, Paul, Jr. "The Frailty of Lemuel Gulliver," in *Essays* [536]
in Literary History Presented to J. Milton French (Edited by

Rudolf Kirk and C. F. Main). New Brunswick, N.J., 1960, pp. 113–125.

The unifying motif of *GT* is "physical injury, pain, and loss." Swift treats "Gulliver the naturalist from a traditional Christian Humanist point of view: what is done to Gulliver physically during his voyages constitutes Swift's major assault on progressivist naturalism."

Geering, R. G. "Swift's Struldbruggs: the Critics Considered," [537]
AUMLA, VII (1957), 5–15.

In Book III Gulliver learns that death is a merciful release. With the Struldbruggs, Swift prepares the way for Book IV. The point of *GT* is that man is an animal capable of reason instead of a reasonable animal.

Geismar, Maxwell. "Gullible Humanity," *New Republic*, [538]
CXXXVI (January 14, 1957), 22.

Discusses the topical, social, Darwinian, and Freudian levels of meaning in *Gulliver*.

Gleeson, Patrick G. "*Gulliver's Travels* as a Version of Gro- [539]
tesque," Unpublished dissertation, University of Washington, 1964.

See *DA*, XXV (1965), 7266.

Goldensohn, Barry. Introduction, *Gulliver's Travels*. New [540]
York, 1962.

Gould, S. H. "Gulliver and the Moons of Mars," *JHI*, VI [541]
(1945), 91–101.

In Book III there is an ironical description of two supposed moons of Mars. Swift's calculations are incorrect.

Gray, James. "The Modernism of Jonathan Swift," *QQ*, LXVII [542]
(1960), 11–17.

Argues that *GT* offers a "prophetic super-diagnosis of humanity's ailments" as applicable today as in 1726. The work is an assault on our pride in reason. We learn that progress in this world is meaningless unless we can abolish the horrors of war, the degradation of man's inhumanity to man, and the assorted cures of unreason.

Greenberg, Robert A. "Swift's *Gulliver's Travels*, Part IV, [543] Chapter III," *Explicator*, XVI (1957), Item 2.
See Ruoff (612).

———. "Gulliver a True Wit," *N&Q*, CCIII, N.S. V (1958), 296. [544] On Swift's treatment of the apple tree shaking incident involving Gulliver and a dwarf in Book II, Chapter 5.

——— (Editor). *Gulliver's Travels: An Annotated Text with* [545] *Critical Essays*. New York, 1961.
Contains previously published essays.

Grennan, Margaret R. "Lilliput and Leprecan: Gulliver and the [546] Irish Tradition," *ELH*, XII (1945), 188–202.
Contends that the adventures in Lilliput and, to a lesser degree, those in Brobdingnag show Swift very close to the Celtic spirit.

Halewood, William H., and Marvin Lynch. "Houyhnhnm *Est* [547] *Animal Rationale*," *JHI*, XXVI (1965), 273–281.
Suggests that Swift fully approved of the Houyhnhnm life of reason and conceived of it as possible for man, as the only realistic standard by which to judge the adequacy of human conduct.

Halewood, William H. "Plutarch in Houyhnhnmland: A [548] Neglected Source of Gulliver's Fourth Voyage," *PQ*, XLIV (1965), 185–194.
Points out similarities between Book IV and Plutarch's "Life" of Lycurgus, the legendary lawgiver of Sparta.

Harlow, Benjamin C. "Houyhnhnmland: A Utopian Satire,"   [549]
McNeese Review, XIII (1962), 44–58.
    The Houyhnhnms are intended as a satirical comment on utopian idealism. Gulliver is taken in by a utopian scheme, so much that he cannot adjust to normal society; Swift is not one whit taken in and satirizes such idealistic visions to expose their ridiculous aspects.

Hart, Jeffrey. "The Ideologue as Artist: Some Notes on *Gulli-*   [550]
ver's Travels," Criticism, II (1960), 125–133.
    Suggests that the relationship between present and past is a central structural principle in GT, Swift's defense of political and social stability.

Heilman, R. B. Introduction, *Gulliver's Travels*. New York,   [551]
1950.
    See Sutherland (633).

Henrion, Pierre. *Jonathan Swift avoue . . . I. Le Secret de Gulli-*   [552]
ver. Versailles, 1963.
    Concerned with proper names as cryptograms. See review in TLS, August 23, 1963, p. 642.

Hitt, Ralph E. "Antiperfectionism as a Unifying Theme in *Gul-*   [553]
liver's Travels," Mississippi Quarterly, XV (1962), 161–169.
    Swift subscribed to what Quintana called "the negative philosophy of history," and GT depicts man's physical, intellectual, and moral deterioration in terms of the passage of time.

Hunting, Robert S. "Gulliver among the Brobdingnagians; a   [554]
Real-life Incident(?)," N&Q, CXCVI (1951), 413.
    A report of 1735 describing a midget.

Jarrell, Mackie L. "The Handwriting of the Lilliputians," PQ,   [555]
XXXVII (1958), 116–119.
    Suggests two sources: William Temple's "Of Heroick Virtue" (1690) and John Ovington's *A Voyage to Suratt* (1696). Disagrees with R. W. Frantz, HLQ, I (1938), 329–334.

Jarrett, James L. "A Yahoo *versus* Jonathan Swift," *WHR*, VIII   [556]
(1954), 195–200.
Considers the intensity and bitterness of Book IV a serious
blemish.

Johnson, Maurice. "Remote Regions of Man's Mind: the Travels   [557]
of Gulliver," *University of Kansas City Review*, XXVII
(1961), 299–303.
Reveals a hidden structure in *GT* by distinguishing the
author from the pretended narrator, who begins his mental
travels comprehending the insignificance of institutions and
becomes increasingly misanthropic until—divided against himself—he "rejects his own humanity."

Joost, Nicholas. "Gulliver and the *Free-thinker*," *MLN*, XLV   [558]
(1950), 197–199.
Argues that Swift took the idea of rope-dancing from Am-
brose Philips' *Free-thinker*, No. 144. See Rosenheim (608).

Kallich, Martin. "Three Ways of Looking at a Horse: Jonathan   [559]
Swift's 'Voyage to the Houyhnhnms' Again," *Criticism*, II
(1960), 107–124.
Reads Book IV as a Christian apologetic, in which Gulliver's praise of the Houyhnhnms amounts to an ironical attack
on the deists and the life of reason. Reviewed together with
Winton (657) by R. S. Crane, *PQ*, XL (1961), 427–430.

Karpman, Benjamin. "A Modern Gulliver: A Study in Copro-   [560]
philia," *Psychoanalytic Review*, XXVI (1949), 162–185; also
260–282.
A presentation of a coprophiliac patient's reactions to his
reading of *Gulliver*.

Kelling, Harold D. "Some Significant Names in *Gulliver's Trav-*   [561]
els," *SP*, XLVIII (1951), 761–778.
Attempts to determine the origin and significance of the
names in two of the imaginary languages and many of the
names not treated before. Related Studies: Baker (489),

Bracher (497), Brandt (498), Clark (513), Cornelius (517), Moore (588), Pons (600), Richer (607), Seeber (617), Seronsy (619).

———. *"Gulliver's Travels*: A Comedy of Humours," *UTQ*, XXI   [562]
(1952), 362–375.
    Views Gulliver as a "humourist"—his humour lying in his ready adaptability to the humours of his hosts.

Kendle, Burton S. "D. H. Lawrence: The Man Who Misunder-   [563]
stood Gulliver," *ELN*, II (1964), 42–46.
    Lawrence's misreading of *Gulliver* and "The Lady's Dressing Room" provides an insight into his own mind and his aim in "The Man Who Loved Islands."

Kermode, Frank. "Yahoos and Houyhnhnms," *N&Q*, CXCV   [564]
(1950), 317–318.
    Concerns the origin of the names Yahoo and Houyhnhnm and mentions possible antecedents.

Kernan, Alvin B. *The Cankered Muse: Satire of the English*   [565]
Renaissance. New Haven, 1959.
    Occasional references to *Gulliver.*

Kieffer, Evelyn T. "A Consideration of the Criticism of Swift's   [566]
Gulliver's Travels, 1890–1960," Unpublished dissertation, University of Southern California, 1964.
    See *DA*, XXV (1965), 5259.

Kimball, Janet G. "A Structural Analysis of the Women in   [567]
Gulliver's Travels," Unpublished dissertation, Western Reserve University, 1962.

Kliger, Samuel. "The Unity of *Gulliver's Travels,*" *MLQ*, VI   [568]
(1945), 401–415.
    An analysis of the structure of *GT* in terms of balance and

contrast of themes. Discusses such motifs as clothing, the return, the happy animal.

Klima, S. "A Possible Source for Swift's Struldbruggs?" *PQ*,   [569]
XLII (1963), 566–569.
Harcouet de Longueville's *Histoire des personnes qui ont vécu plusieurs siècles.* See Peterson (599).

Kott, J. "Przeklady Gulliwera," *Zeszyty Wroclawskie,* Num-   [570]
ber 4 (1948), 68–72.

Landa, Louis A. Introduction, *Gulliver's Travels.* Boston, 1960.   [571]

Lawlor, John. "Radical Satire and the Realistic Novel," *Essays*   [572]
and Studies, N.S. VIII (1955), 58–75.
Concerns the evolution of the character of Gulliver.

Leyburn, Ellen D. "Certain Problems of Allegorical Satire in   [573]
Gulliver's Travels," HLQ, XIII (1950), 161–189.
Concerns the work's allegorical intention and significance.
See Leyburn (574).

———. *Satiric Allegory: Mirror of Man.* New Haven, 1956, pp.   [574]
71–91.
Reviewed by R. C. Elliott, *MLN,* LXXII (1957), 453–456;
see Leyburn (573).

———. "Gulliver's Clothes," *Satire News Letter,* I (1964), 35–40.   [575]
See Schuster (616).

Livingston, D. A. "Yeahohs and Mating 'Possums'," *Western*   [576]
Folklore, XVII (1958), 55–56.
Suggests that a previous note on a tale dealing with "hairy
women" (*Western Folklore,* XVI [1957], 48–51) was influ-
enced by Gulliver's encounter with the Yahoos.

Longhurst, John E. "Fielding and Swift in Mexico," *Modern*   [577]
     Language Journal, XXXVI (1952), 186–187.
     Spanish versions of *Gulliver's Travels* came to Mexico soon
     after 1800. In June 1803 the work, along with *Tom Jones*, was
     sent by the secretary of the Inquisition in Mexico City to the
     nearby Dominican monastery for study by two friars whose
     opinions are printed.

McAleer, John J. "Gulliver at Greenwich," *English Record*,   [578]
     XII (1961), 38–39.
     Suggests that an allusion in *GT*, Book I, to bowling-green
     at Greenwich may be to "Bo[w]lingbroke at Greenwich,"
     where certain amorous adventures lost him the Lord Trea-
     surership when Anne learned of them.

McNelis, James I. "The Education of Lemuel Gulliver: a Study   [579]
     of the Unity of *Gulliver's Travels*." Unpublished dissertation,
     Columbia University, 1954.
     See *DA*, XIV (1954), 2337.

——. Introduction, *Journey of Niels Klim to the World Un-*   [580]
     derground (Edited by J. I. McNelis). Lincoln, Nebraska,
     1960, pp. vii–xxxi.
     Discusses Swift's relation to Holberg.

Mack, Maynard. "The Muse of Satire," *YR*, XLI (1951), 80–92.   [581]
     Refers to the repeated error of seeing Gulliver's views in
     Houyhnhnmland as identical with Swift's.

——. "*Gulliver's Travels*," in *English Masterpieces*, V: *The*   [582]
     Augustans (2nd edition). Englewood Cliffs, N.J., 1961, pp.
     14–16.
     An excellent introductory essay.

Mackenzie, Aline. "Another Note on *Gulliver's Travels* (Pt. I,   [583]
     Ch. III)," *N&Q*, CXCIII (1948), 533–538.
     Suggests that Swift draws on the popular entertainments of

rope-dancing and the Harlequinades as a means of satire in the passage where the Emperor of Lilliput entertains. Describes Swift's delight in popular spectacles and buffoonery.

Merle, Robert. "Les Desseins de Gulliver," *Revue de Paris*,   [584]
   April 1959, pp. 15–23.
   Gulliver is every middle-class, informed European man, but he never invokes his saviour; Swift was a dean in public, a skeptic in his study. Swift's borrowings are noteworthy: he takes material from manuals of navigation and misapplies it, pillages Cyrano de Bergerac's voyage to the moon, and leans on *The Arabian Nights* for the fondling of Gulliver by Brobdingnagian ladies, but he adds disgust to moral condemnation. The humiliation of pride to Swift is an end in itself.

Merrill, C. F. "Some Reflections on *Gulliver's Travels*," *The*   [585]
   Mathematics Teacher, LIV (December 1961), 620–625.
   A study of the mathematics employed by Swift reveals that in creating his world in miniature, he has used a proportion of twelve to one, that he "had little appreciation of the purer and less practical aspects of mathematics and science," and that he incorporated several "scientific inconsistencies" in his work.

Monk, Samuel. "The Pride of Lemuel Gulliver," *SR*, LXIII   [586]
   (1955), 48–71.
   Swift's grim joke is that Gulliver himself is the supreme instance of a creature smitten with pride. Sees the *Travels* as a satire on the physical, political, intellectual, and moral aspects of man—"the work of a Christian humanist and moralist."

Moog, Florence. "Gulliver Was a Bad Biologist," *Scientific*   [587]
   American, CLXXIX (1948), 52–55.
   Presents amusing scientific calculations proving that the Brobdingnagians are too big and the Lilliputians too small to be able to exist in reality.

Moore, John R. "The Yahoos of the African Travellers," *N&Q*,   [588]
   CXCV (1950), 182–185.
   As early as 1732 an African travel book gives an account of

an inland people called Yahoos who were once Christians. To suggest the degeneration of religious faith and a national culture, the African Yahoos were perfect. With a tradition of a long lost civilization these people were presently living in slavery and personal filth and were possessed with inordinate lust. Related Studies: Baker (489), Bracher (497), Brandt (498), Clark (513), Cornelius (517), Kelling (561), Pons (600), Richer (607), Seeber (617), Seronsy (619).

Morris, Harry C. "*The Dialogues of Hylas and Philonous* as a   [589] Source in *Gulliver's Travels*," MLN, LXX (1955), 175–177.

Mortenson, Robert. "A Note on the Revision of *Gulliver's*   [590] *Travels*," *Library Chronicle of the University of Pennsylvania*, XXVIII (1962), 26–28.
On the sharpening of a reference to the law in Book IV, 5.

Murray, W. A. "Mr. Roland M. Frye's Article on Swift's Yahoo," JHI, XV (1954), 599–601.   [591]
See Frye (535).

Nemser, William. "Linguistic Economy in Lagado," *History of*   [592] *Ideas News Letter*, I (1955), 7–10.

Neumeyer, Peter F. "Franz Kafka and Jonathan Swift: A Symbiosis," *Dalhousie Review*, XLV (1965), 60–65.   [593]
Kafka takes Swift at face value and attributes the views of Gulliver and the Lilliputians to Swift himself. See Adams (488).

Newman, J. R. "Commentary on the Island of Laputa," in *The*   [594] *World of Mathematics*. New York, 1956, Vol. IV, pp. 2210–2213.
Discovers Laputa "by no means devoid of the superlative literary and philosophic qualities that have won the *Travels*

a place among the masterpieces of imagination and social commentary;" sees the voyage as a satire on pedantry in science and learning.

Nicolson, Marjorie H. *Voyages to the Moon*. New York, 1948, [595] pp. 189–195.
Discusses Swift's Flying Island in terms of its sources.

Papajewski, Helmut. "Swift and Berkeley," *Anglia*, LXXVII [596] (1959), 29–53.
Discusses Berkeley's *New Theory of Vision* and Swift's use of it as a source of his skeptical view of man's greatness; minimizes Berkeley's influence. See Wasiolek (649).

Parsons, Coleman O. "The Background of *The Mysterious* [597] *Stranger*," *American Literature*, XXXII (1960), 55–74.
Concerns the influence of *Gulliver* on Twain.

Partridge, Eric. "Brobdingnag and Lilliput," in *Here, There* [598] *and Everywhere: Essays Upon Language*. New York, 1950, pp. 126–130.
Discusses proper names in *Gulliver* and their effect upon the English language.

Peterson, Leland D. "On the Keen Appetite for Perpetuity of [599] Life," *ELN*, I (1964), 265–267.
The Struldbrugg episode represents Swift's attack on the scientific eagerness to prolong life. See Klima (569).

Pons, Emile. "Swift, Créateur Linguistique: À propos du Lilli- [600] putien," in "Langues Imaginaires et Langage Secret chez Swift," *Cashiers du Sud*, XLVI (1958), 31–39.
Swift used Rabelais' method of invented imaginary languages. Related Studies: Baker (489), Bracher (497), Brandt (498), Clark (513), Cornelius (517), Kelling (561), Moore (588), Richer (607), Seeber (617), Seronsy (619).

Preu, James. "Swift's Influence on Godwin's Doctrine of An-   [601]
archism," *JHI*, XV (1954), 371–383.
  Discusses the influence of Book IV upon the Utopian society in *Political Justice*. See Preu (287) and (288).

———. "The Case of the Mysterious Manuscript," *English Jour-*   [602]
nal, LII (1963), 579–586.
  The true meaning of *GT* remains an enigma; the case of
the mysterious manuscript has not yet been solved. Discusses
"ambiguities which stir up scholarly controversy."

Quennell, Peter. Introduction, *Gulliver's Travels*. London,   [603]
1952.

Quintana, Ricardo. Introduction, *Gulliver's Travels*. New   [604]
York, 1958.

Reichard, Hugo M. "Gulliver the Pretender," *Papers on Eng-*   [605]
lish Language and Literature, I (1965), 316–326.
  Swift is doing what Hobbes apparently did before him—
reading the attributes of advanced society back into the state
of nature. Above all, it is Gulliver's finesse as a pretender
which enables Swift to express this and thereby to make the
satire seem oppressively unanswerable on its own terms.

Reiss, Edmund. "The Importance of Swift's Glubbdubdrib Epi-   [606]
sode," *JEGP*, LIX (1960), 223–228.
  An important step in Gulliver's education and a direct link
between Books II and IV.

Richer, Jean. "Swift au Pays de Kabbale," in "Langues Imagi-   [607]
naires et Langage Secret chez Swift," *Cashiers du Sud*, XLVI
(1958), 5–14.
  Yahoo is based on the German *Jauche*, which is related to
the Greek *ichor* and various Slavic words. This European ex-
tension of the word makes it suitable for a semicabbalistic
usage. *Yahoo* thus represents "man in a state of complete

degradation, bathing in the ordure of the seven deadly sins, feeding on his own vomit and finding it delectable." Similar Anglo-Germanic word play and European linguistic affinities are discovered throughout the Houyhnhnm language. Related Studies: Baker (489), Bracher (497), Brandt (498), Clark (513), Cornelius (517), Kelling (561), Moore (588), Pons (600), Seeber (617), Seronsy (619).

Rosenheim, Edward W., Jr. "A 'Source' for the Rope-dancing [608] in *Gulliver's Travels*," *PQ*, XXXI (1952), 208–211.
    Argues against Philips' *Free-thinker* (1719) as the source. See Joost (558).

———. "The Fifth Voyage of Lemuel Gulliver: A Footnote," [609] *MP*, LX (1962), 103–119.
    A discussion of Book IV.

Ross, John F. Introduction, *Gulliver's Travels*. New York, 1953. [610]

Rossi, Matti M. "Notes on the Eighteenth-Century German [611] Translation of Swift's *Gulliver's Travels*," *Library Chronicle of the University of Pennsylvania*, XXV (1959), 84–88.

Ruoff, James E. "Swift's *Gulliver's Travels*, Part IV, Chapter [612] III," *Explicator*, XV (1956), Item 20.
    See Greenberg (543).

Sampson, Edward C. "*Gulliver's Travels*: Book III," *N&Q*, [613] CXCVI (1951), 474–475.
    On Swift's debt to William Gilbert's *De Magnete*.

Sauers, Philip. "Wisdom is a Nut; or the Idols of Jonathan [614] Swift," in *If By Your Art: Testament to Percival Hunt* (Edited by A. L. Starrett). Pittsburg, 1949, pp. 71–95.
    Chiefly an interpretation of Book III.

Schucking, Levin L. "Gullivers Reise zu den Guten Pferden," [615]
in *Sitzungsberiche der Bayerischen Akademie der Wissen-
schaften.* Munchen, 1953.

Schuster, Sister M. Faith, O.S.B. "Clothes Philosophy in *Gul-* [616]
liver's Travels," *American Benedictine Review*, XV (1964),
316–326.
A Christian interpretation of *GT*. See Leyburn (575).

Seeber, Edward. "Ideal Languages in the French and English [617]
Imaginary Voyages," *PMLA*, LX (1945), 586–597.
Related Studies: Baker (489), Bracher (497), Brandt (498),
Clark (513), Cornelius (517), Kelling (561), Moore (588),
Pons (600), Richer (607), Seronsy (619).

Seelye, John D. "Hobbes' *Leviathan* and the Giantism Complex [618]
in the First Book of *Gulliver's Travels*," *JEGP*, LX (1961),
228–239.
Suggests that Book I of *GT*, in which Swift extends
Hobbes' imagery, amounts to a satire on Hobbesian doctrine. The feud between giant and pygmies expresses "a basic
tension between the needs of the individual and the demands
of the state"—a reminder of England's injustice to Ireland.

Seronsy, Cecil C. "Some Proper Names in *Gulliver's Travels*," [619]
N&Q, CCII, N.S. IV (1957), 470–471.
Laputa and *Lilliput* are derived from Latin *puto* (I think);
hence *Laputa* "the country of the thinkers" and *Lilliput* "the
country of little minds." *Gulliver* suggests not only *gullible*
but also "truth" (cf. *ver*); hence *Gulliver* "the dupe of truth."
See particularly Brandt (498). The following are related
studies: Baker (489), Bracher (497), Clark (513), Cornelius
(517), Kelling (561), Moore (588), Pons (600), Richer (607),
Seeber (617).

———. "Sir Politic Would-Be in Laputa," *ELN*, I (1963), 17–24. [620]
Similarities between Jonson's character and Laputan states-
men.

Shaw, Sheila. "Early English Editions of the *Arabian Nights*: [621] Their Value to Eighteenth Century Literary Scholarship," *Muslim World*, XLIX (1959), 232–238.
Concerns the influence of the *Arabian Nights* on *GT*.

Sherburn, George. Introduction, *Gulliver's Travels*. New York, [622] 1950.

———. "Errors Concerning the Houyhnhnms," *MP*, LVI (1958), [623] 92–97.
To equate reason and deism is false because Swift himself accepted reason in religion. The church is untouched in *GT*. Why use horses if they are to satirize deists? Notes Swift's fondness for horses in a letter to Ford. The Houyhnhnms represent Swift's clearly imperfect concept of the "perfection of nature." See Ehrenpreis (525).

Slepian, Barry. "The Publication History of Faulkner's Edi- [624] tion of *Gulliver's Travels*," *PBSA*, LVII (1963), 219–221.

Smith, Raymond J., Jr. "Swift's Art in *Gulliver's Travels*," [625] Unpublished dissertation, University of Wisconsin, 1961.
See *DA*, XXII (1961), 861.

———. "The 'Character' of Lemuel Gulliver," *TSL*, X (1965), [626] 133–140.
Swift's basic intent is to manipulate Gulliver as an instrument, a construct properly shorn of all novelistic ego, a creature to whom notions of development are irrelevant.

Stanzel, Franz K. "*Gulliver's Travels*: Satire, Utopie, Dys- [627] topie," *Die Moderne Sprachen*, VII (1963), 106–116.

Stavrou, C. N. "Gulliver's Voyage to the Land of the Dub- [628] liners," *SAQ*, LIX (1960), 490–499.
Believes that *Ulysses* has significant affinities with *Gulliver*.

Steensma, Robert C. "Swift's Model for Lord Munodi," *N&Q*, [629]
CCX, N.S. XII (1965), 216–217.
Suggests Sir William Temple.

Steeves, Harrison R. "Saeva Indignatio," in *Before Jane Austen:* [630]
The Shaping of the English Novel in the Eighteenth Century.
New York, 1965, pp. 43–52.
Suggests that *Gulliver* introduced the spirit of poetic satire
into English fiction, put vitality into hitherto humdrum prose
narrative, proved the potential interest of trivial circum-
stance and incident, and combined adventure with everyday
feeling, thinking, and acting.

Stone, Edward. "Swift and the Horses: Misanthropy or Com- [631]
edy?" *MLQ*, X (1949), 367–376.
Book IV is essentially comic not misanthropic.

Suits, Conrad. "The Role of the Horses in 'A Voyage to the [632]
Houyhnhnms'," *UTQ*, XXXIV (1965), 118–132.
Suggests that "Gulliver was not mad and therefore not a
comic figure; rather that he made valid inferences about
human nature from the evidence before him and so was as
sane as his creator, or as you or I for that matter."

Sutherland, John N. "A Reconsideration of Gulliver's Third [633]
Voyage," *SP*, LIV (1957), 45–52.
Suggests that Voyage III is a strong and necessary part of
GT by showing its internal unity and by showing that it is
essential to the total pattern of the *Travels*. See Heilman
(551).

Sutherland, W. O. S., Jr. "Satire and the Use of History: Gul- [634]
liver's Third Voyage," in *The Art of the Satirist: Essays on
the Satire of Augustan England.* Austin, Texas, 1965, pp.
107–128.
An informed treatment of Book III.

Tallman, Warren. "Swift's Fool: A Comment Upon Satire in [635] *Gulliver's Travels*," *Dalhousie Review*, XL (1961), 470–478.
Gulliver is "Swift's fool," approaching all situations in his travels with reliance on merely human qualities; nowhere does he entreat divine guidance or protection. Gulliver's naiveté is the foolishness of those who find their objects of worship here below. His comic madness is Swift's exhortation to lift one's eyes.

Taylor, Aline M. "Cyrano de Bergerac and Gulliver's 'Voyage [636] to Brobdingnag'," *TSE*, V (1955), 83–102.
Argues that Swift's debt to the *Histoire de la Lune* in Book II has been exaggerated.

———. "Sights and Monsters and Gulliver's 'Voyage to Brob- [637] dingnag'," *TSE*, VII (1957), 29–82.
On Swift's use of contemporary materials.

Taylor, Dick, Jr. "Gulliver's Pleasing Visions: Self-deception [638] as Major Theme in *Gulliver's Travels*," *TSE*, XII (1962), 7–61.
Isolates Gulliver's trait of self-deception or self-delusion to suggest that it constitutes the major theme, that it is the focus of the whole work.

Tilton, John W. "*Gulliver's Travels* as a Work of Art," *BuR*, [639] VIII (1959), 246–259.
Sees the *Travels* as a unified work of art in which the *voyage* genre is employed to demonstrate the logical development of Gulliver's education and developing characterization.

———. "Generic Criticisms of *Gulliver's Travels*: An Appraisal [640] Based on a Study of Swift's Use of the Elements of Fiction," Unpublished dissertation, Pennsylvania State University, 1962.
See *DA*, XXIII (1963), 4366.

Todd, W. B. "The Text of *Gulliver's Travels*," *Library*, 5th [641]
series, IX (1954), 135–136.
See Williams (650) and (651); also Danchin (521).

Tracy, Clarence. "The Unity of *Gulliver's Travels*," *QQ*, [642]
LXVIII (1962), 597–609.
Suggests that Swift neither satirizes nor idealizes the Houyhnhnms, but he very powerfully satirizes the man who, like
Gulliver, makes a fool of himself by mistaking them for a
viable human ideal. See a review by H. K. Miller, *PQ*, XLI
(1962), 632.

Traugott, John. "A Voyage to Nowhere with Thomas More [643]
and Jonathan Swift: *Utopia* and 'The Voyage to the Houyhnhnms'," *SR*, LXIX (1961), 534–565.
Concerns similarities rather than influences.

———. "Swift's Allegory: The Yahoo and the Man-of-Mode," [644]
UTQ, XXXIII (1963), 1–18.
Finds Swift often associating modishness with degeneracy.

Tuveson, Ernest. "Swift: the Dean as Satirist," *UTQ*, XXII [645]
(1953), 368–375.
Considering his religious commitment, Swift could not have
offered the Houyhnhnms as his ideal. Interprets Book IV
in the light of the doctrine of original sin, viewing the horses
as representing "unfallen rational beings" and Gulliver's emu-
lation of them as comic.

Tyne, James L., S.J. "Gulliver's Maker and Gullibility," *Criti-* [646]
cism, VII (1965), 151–167.
In showing man what he essentially and existentially is,
Swift ridiculed pride, but he did this to awaken a humility
which is the beginning of wisdom.

Ure, Peter. "Laputans and Eleutheri: Swift and the *Vindicator* [647]
of the Clergy," *N&Q*, CCII, N.S. IV (1957), 164–167.
Swift may have derived the idea for the banquet in the

Palace of the King of Laputa from an anonymous attack on Eachard in 1672.

Wahlund, Per Erik. *En Gulliverkommentar*. Stockholm, 1955. [648]

Wasiolek, Edward. "Relativity in *Gulliver's Travels*," *PQ*, [649] XXXVII (1958), 110–116.

Suggests that "the idea of relativity, borrowed consciously or unconsciously from Berkeley, is for Swift a structural device that informs his central satiric purpose, the attack on man's pride." See Papajewski (596).

Williams, Sir Harold. *The Text of "Gulliver's Travels."* Cam- [650] bridge, England, 1952.

Reviews: *TLS*, December 19, 1952, p. 297; I. Ehrenpreis, *PQ*, XXXII (1953), 297–299; L. Landa, *RES*, VI (1955), 322–323; see also the following exchange between William B. Todd and Harold Williams: Todd, *Library*, 5th series, VIII (1953), 280–282; Williams, *ibid.*, 283–284; Todd, *Library*, 5th series, IX (1954), 135–136; Williams, *ibid.*, 270. See also Danchin (521), Williams (651).

———. "*Gulliver's Travels*," *TLS*, January 9, 1952, p. 25. [651]

A reply to a review in *TLS*, December 19, 1952, p. 297. See Williams (650), Todd (641), Danchin (521).

Williams, Kathleen. "Gulliver's Voyage to the Houyhnhnms," [652] *ELH*, XVIII (1951), 275–286.

Suggests that the Houyhnhnms, "far from being a model of perfection, are intended to show the inadequacy of the life of reason."

———. "*Animal Rationis Capax*: A Study of Certain Aspects of [653] Swift's Imagery," *ELH*, XXI (1954), 193–207.

———. "Swift's Laputans and 'Mathematica'," *N&Q*, CCVIII, [654] N.S. X (1963), 216–217.

Discusses the relationship to the emblematic figure in C. Giarda's *Icones Symbolicae* (1626).

Wilson, James R. "Swift's *Alazon*," *Studia Neophilologia*, XXX [655] (1958), 153–164.
Views Gulliver as the sympathetic imposter who is intended by Swift to dupe the reader.

———. "Swift, the Psalmist, and the Horse," *TSL*, III (1958), [656] 17–23.
Sees the psalmist's warning—"A horse is counted but a vain thing to save a man"—as the key to Book IV.

Winton, Calhoun. "Conversion on the Road to Houyhnhnm- [657] land," *SR*, LXVIII (1960), 20–33.
Interprets Book IV as a Christian allegory. Reviewed together with Kallich (559) by R. S. Crane, *PQ*, XL (1961), 427–430.

Zall, Paul M. "Lolita and Gulliver," *Satire News Letter*, III [658] (1965), 33–37.

Zimansky, Curtis A. "Gulliver, Yahoos, and Critics," *CE*, [659] XXVII (1965), 45–49.
Suggests "that a too rapid use of the historical approach can lead to error, that history can be used to reinforce a prejudice, or can combine with critical technique to obscure what is clear; that on the other hand a rigorous use of the history of ideas can rectify error and permit us to extend critical dimensions."

See (58), (61), (76), (84), (96), (104), (117), (128), (129), (140), (164), (168), (175), (177), (179), (180), (182), (183), (184), (190), (199), (200), (204), (205), (206), (207), (208), (210), (211), (212), (215), (227), (229), (232), (233), (234), (238), (244), (245), (251), (252), (254), (263), (273), (275), (280), (282), (287), (288), (289), (290), (293), (294), (295), (300), (303), (306), (307), (309), (314), (324), (328), (331), (332), (333), (335), (340), (342), (343), (344), (454), (478).

Index of Authors

References are to items, not to pages

A

Ackerman, Catherine, 84
Acworth, Bernard, 61
Adams, Percy G., 487
Adams, Robert M., 488
Aden, John M., 389
Alexander, Jean, 164
Allen, Robert J., 293, 428
Anderson, P., 76
Andreasen, N. J. C., 395
Arnold, Aerol, 303
Atherton, James S., 165, 166
Atkins, J. W. H., 167
Axelrad, José, 132

B

Babcock, R. W., 62
Baker, Donald C., 396, 447
Baker, Frank, 63
Baker, Sheridan, 489
Ball, Albert, 490
Banks, Loy O., 491
Barker, Elizabeth, 455
Barnds, William J., 64
Barrett, William, 65
Barroll, J. Leeds, 492, 493
Barzun, Jacques, 168
Bateson, F. W., 347
Battestin, Martin C., 303
Beaumont, Charles A., 169, 170, 448
Beckett, J. C., 58ix, 86, 109, 114, 128, 171, 444
Benjamin, Edwin B., 494
Bennett, Hiram R., 66
Béranger, J., 172, 532
Bernard, F. V., 469
Bewley, Marius, 348
Block, Edward A., 495

B (continued — second column)

Bloom, Allan, 496
Bond, Donald F., 17
Bond, Richmond P., 470, 471
Bottome, Phyllis, 67
Boyce, Benjamin, 486
Bracher, Frederick, 497
Brady, Frank, 86, 109, 173, 413, 444
Brain, Sir Walter Russell, 68
Brandt, E. H., 498
Bredvold, Louis I., 174, 175
Brengle, R. L., 176, 335
Briggs, H. E., 177
Brinton, Henry C., 499
Brookes, T. H., 69
Brown, James, 178
Brown, Norman O., 179
Brown, T. J., 70
Brown, William J., 500
Bruckmann, Patricia, 501
Bryant, Donald C., 169
Buchan, H., 54
Bullitt, John M., 180, 294
Bullough, Geoffrey, 86, 115
Burgess, C. F., 181
Burian, Orhan, 502
Burns, Wayne, 503
Butt, John, 182, 342
Buxton, George, 183
Byers, John R., Jr., 504

C

Cable, Chester H., 403
Calderwood, James L., 426
Calkin, Homer L., 444
Calkins, Ernest E., 505
Callan, Norman, 294
Canseliet, Eugène, 184
Carnochan, W. B., 506, 607, 508
Carroll, John, 185

105

Notes

Notes

Notes

Notes